D0852460

Yours to Keep
Withdrawn/ABCL

RIO GRANDE VALLEY
LIBRARY SYSTEM LG

Turkey

Yours to Keep

Withdrawn/ABCL

3 9075 02743349 6

Turkey

BY TAMRA ORR

*Enchantment of the World
Second Series*

Children's Press®

A Division of Scholastic Inc.

NEW YORK   TORONTO   LONDON   AUCKLAND   SYDNEY
MEXICO CITY   NEW DELHI   HONG KONG
DANBURY, CONNECTICUT

RIO GRANDE VALLEY LG
LIBRARY SYSTEM

Frontispiece: Turkish cherry drink seller

Consultant: Dr. Sabri Sayari, Director, Institute of Turkish Studies, Georgetown University, Washington, D.C.

Please note: All statistics are as up-to-date as possible at the time of publication.

Book production by Herman Adler Design

Library of Congress Cataloging-in-Publication Data

Orr, Tamra.
    Turkey / by Tamra Orr.
        p. cm. — (Enchantment of the world. Second series)
    Includes bibliographical references and index.
    ISBN 0-516-22679-7
    1. Turkey—Juvenile literature. [1. Turkey.] I. Title. II. Series.
DR440 .O77 2003
956.1—dc21   2002001590

© 2003 by Children's Press, a Division of Scholastic Inc.
All rights reserved. Published simultaneously in Canada.
Printed in the United States of America.

CHILDREN'S PRESS and associated logos are trademarks and or registered
trademarks of Grolier Publishing Co., Inc. SCHOLASTIC and associated logos
are trademarks and or registered trademarks of Scholastic Inc.
1 2 3 4 5 6 7 8 9 10 R 12 11 10 09 08 07 06 05 04 03

Turkey

Contents

Cover photo:
Blue Mosque,
Istanbul, Turkey

Cappadocia

Kurdish woman and children

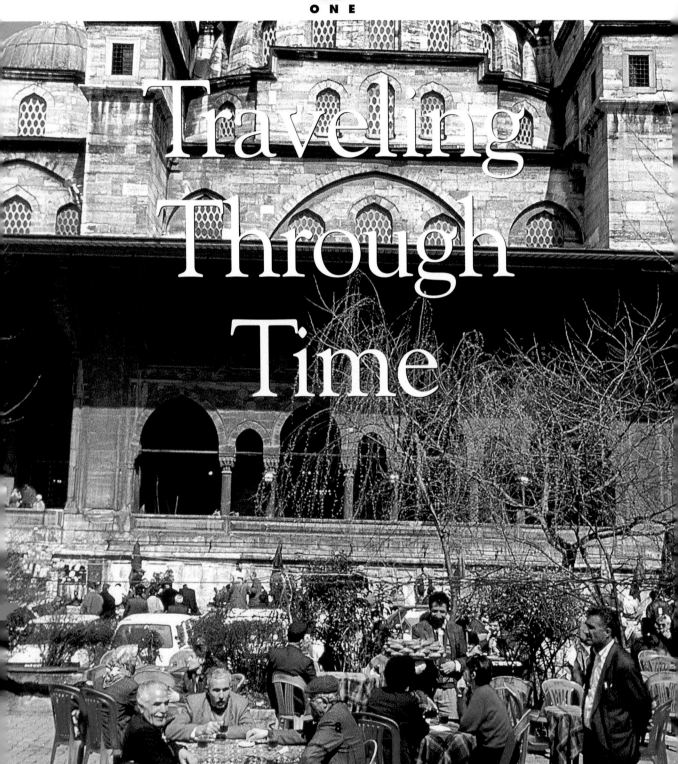

Traveling Through Time

H ELLO! I FINALLY MADE IT TO TURKEY. IT WAS A LONG journey, but it was definitely worth it. This week has been incredible as I begin to learn about this fascinating nation. It is such a mixture of cultures. I glance one way and see a high-rise apartment building, and then I turn around and see a mosque that is hundreds of years old. Businessmen in suits and ties brush past me, and then I find myself walking behind a group of women wearing traditional headscarves and long dresses. It's like traveling through time in an instant.

Each morning, the *muezzin* has awakened me. As soon as the first light of dawn appears, he calls people to prayer from the *mosque*, an Islamic house of prayer, over a loudspeaker. He does this five times a day to remind everyone! People wash their hands, feet, and faces outside the mosque before going inside to pray.

It is hard to know where to start when touring this country. It is divided into eight basic regions, and there are sites I just have to see in each one of them. I will certainly want to spend time exploring the Egyptian Spice Market and the Topkapi Palace and Treasury. I can't wait to see the 84-carat diamond there!

Opposite: **The seventeenth-century Yeni Mosque is the backdrop to a modern-day outdoor café in Istanbul.**

Bags of spices at an Istanbul spice market

Remains of the *Yassiada* wreck can be viewed at the Bodrum Museum of Underwater Archaeology.

My list of museums to visit keeps growing longer. I want to see the Bodrum Museum of Underwater Archaeology and the Independence War Museum and Museum of Anatolian Civilizations in Ankara. Of course, I am also going to take some time for relaxation. I plan to enjoy the beaches on the Mediterranean and the Aegean Sea coasts. There are quite a few spots to relax and enjoy the incredibly good weather. I was just told that from these beaches you can rent a yacht and a guide for the day and see some extraordinary sites. Would you

One of Turkey's many beaches

believe that there are entire cities under the water on Aperlae and Kekova Islands? An earthquake sank many of the buildings and homes below the water's surface.

I hope to put my new camera to use by taking pictures of Mount Ararat, in the far-eastern part of the country. At 16,949 feet (5,166 meters) tall, it is supposed to be an incredible sight. I also want to take pictures of the carved heads of the ancient gods and kings up on Nemrut Mountain, which is not as far east. They say the best time to go is just as the sun comes up and hits the red rocks. I'm sure I will use up even more film when I go to several of Turkey's many national parks. The number of flowers and animals they have here is so vast! I want to take pictures of everything so that I can share it with all of you when I return.

You would love the food here. I know I do! I have learned to eat lamb in all different kinds of ways—from stuffed into bread to *shish kabob*. I have discovered that I really like drinking tea. Everyone drinks it. My favorite treat so far, however, is Turkish delight, a type of candy. It's delicious, and it doesn't taste anything like the kind they make in the United States. I'll try to bring some back home with me.

Do you think that I should bring back a genuine Turkish carpet? Each one is handmade and dyed with incredible colors and designs. The Grand Bazaar in Istanbul has more carpets than I could ever have imagined. Each one is covered with different symbols, and I am slowly learning from the merchants what they mean. The people at the hotel have warned me that I shouldn't really show that I like any one particular carpet.

On Nemrut Mountain, the huge statues collapsed as a result of earthquakes in the region.

A Turkish rug salesman displays his rugs to a group of tourists.

Opposite: **The Grand Bazaar is a good place to shop and to practice speaking Turkish!**

Instead, I am supposed to act like I am not interested in any of them and keep asking questions. They say I can get a better price this way. It's called haggling. That should be interesting!

I have learned a lot about a man named Atatürk. His portrait is everywhere, so I started asking some questions. People were quite surprised that I hadn't heard of him before. He is the person responsible for founding the Republic of Turkey. He was an amazing man—he did more to change his country than almost any leader I have ever heard of. I want to know more about him, so I am going to be sure and visit Anitkabir, Atatürk's mausoleum, in the capital city of Ankara.

I have developed a new respect for architecture here, too. Both the Green Mosque and the Blue Mosque are beautiful, and the Hagia Sophia is breathtaking. Did you know that when you visit a mosque you can't wear shorts? You also have to remove your shoes and carry them with you. Women are expected to cover their arms, legs, heads, and shoulders. I am finding out all about basilicas, which are churches, and minarets, the spires on mosques.

Believe it or not, I have already picked up some Turkish words and phrases. Some of the people here speak English, but they are delighted when a visitor says something to them in their native language. It's like I have done something miraculous! I have learned to say simple things like "good morning" and "thank you." "*Onun fiyati ne?*" means "How much is that?" and "*Çok pahali, alamam*" means "I can't afford that." I bought a shirt at the Grand Bazaar the other day, and the vendor said "*Güle güle giyin*" to me. When I asked what that meant, I found out it translates to "Wear it laughingly," or simply, "Wear it in happiness." Isn't that a wonderful thing to hear when you buy some clothing?

I must go. I am off to a day of sightseeing and perhaps even a trip to the ancient city of Troy, which I have heard so much about. When I get back tonight, I am planning to check out several of the nightclubs and dance places so my day will end with music and fun!

I know that the next three weeks will fly by as I continue to explore this unique country, where the past and the present seem to merge together. I will keep writing letters home to you and taking pictures so that you can share in the experience, too. Here's to all of my new discoveries and explorations!

Allahaismarladik! (That means "goodbye.")

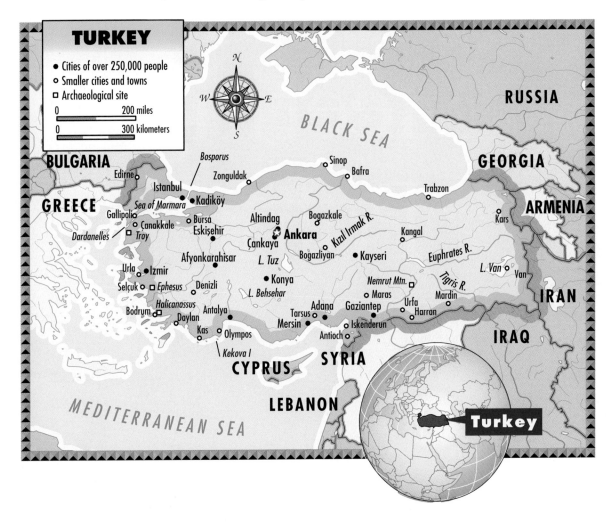

A Unique Meeting Point

TURKEY IS A REMARKABLE COUNTRY, AND THE LONGER A person explores it, the more fascinating it seems. A quick look at a map shows one main reason it is such an interesting place: it is actually located on two continents, close to where the three continents of Asia, Europe, and Africa come together. In the world of geography, this is quite distinctive! About 3 percent of the country lies within Europe and is called Eastern Thrace. The other 97 percent of Turkey is located in Asia and is called Anatolia, or Asia Minor.

Opposite: **A view across the fields and mountains of Turkey**

This aerial view of Turkey shows the country's unique position between Europe and Asia.

Unlike some of the lands that neighbor it, Turkey is not only a Middle Eastern country. It shares a lot with Europe. In addition, Turkey is considered to be one of the world's cradles of civilization. Over the centuries, it has given birth to many civilizations, religions, empires, and states.

At the Borders

Turkey is shaped like a rectangle and is just a little smaller than the U.S. states of Texas and Louisiana combined. It is similar to a peninsula, which would be surrounded on three sides by water. To Turkey's north is the Black Sea; to the south is the Mediterranean Sea; and to the west is the Aegean Sea. Three bodies of water—the Bosporus Strait, the Sea of Marmara, and the Dardanelles Strait—divide the continents of Europe and Asia from each other within Turkey. With all of this water, Turkey has a great deal of coastline—almost

Although rugged and left to nature, this section of the coastline attracts sunbathers.

Ford of the Cow

The name *Bosporus* means "Ford of the Cow" in Greek. According to legend, the Bosporous Strait got its name when the goddess Hera sent a swarm of gnats to irritate another goddess named Io. In order to escape her tormentor, Io swam the strait and gave it the name.

In 1914, Turkey lost control of the Bosporus. Then, in 1936, the Montreux Convention, which regulated the passage of ships through the Bosporus and the Dardanelles Straits, gave back military control of it to Turkey. At that time, about 100 to 150 ships passed through the strait each year. Now that number is fast approaching 50,000 per year, thanks to the exportation of oil. A bridge links the Asian and European sides of the strait.

4,474 miles (7,200 kilometers) of it. Some parts of the coast are beautiful beaches that attract thousands of vacationers each year; other parts are untouched and wild. Turkey also has a number of large saltwater lakes and numerous rivers, including the Euphrates and the Tigris Rivers.

The Black Sea Runs Over

In the summer of 1998, it just kept raining in eastern Turkey. As reported on August 12, the Black Sea finally overflowed and flooded the area. Ten people were killed, dozens were missing, and more than fifty homes were destroyed. The rains came again in December of that year. Hundreds of people had to be evacuated, and a hotel collapsed.

The portions of Turkey that aren't touching water are the bordering countries of Greece, Bulgaria, Georgia, Armenia, Iran, Iraq, Azerbaijan, and Syria. Greece and Bulgaria are in Europe, and the other countries are in Asia.

The Eight Regions

Turkey can be divided geographically into eight main regions, each with its own landscape, history, and flavor. They are Thrace, the Black Sea, the Marmara and the Aegean, the Mediterranean, Western Anatolia, Central Anatolia, Eastern Anatolia, and Southeastern Anatolia.

The small region of Eastern Thrace has rolling hills and fertile grasslands. It is perfect for farming and grazing. This region produces quite a bit of maize (a type of corn), wine, and tobacco in fields stretching all the way to the horizon. In the cold winter months, herds of sheep can be seen wandering the slopes as shepherds watch nearby.

The northern Black Sea region is different from the rest of the country. Rain falls heavily on a regular basis, and cows wander through the pastures. The western part of the coast remains rather undeveloped, and people there mainly live in noncommercial fishing towns.

The Marmara and the Aegean is an important agricultural region where groves of olives and other crops fill the landscape. It is wet and green, with rich soil. The Marmara includes the bustling city of Bursa, the first capital of the Ottoman Empire. Because of Marmara's closeness to the thriving city of Istanbul, industry is spreading into this region.

Meadows and hills of the
eastern section of the Black
Sea region

Ruins of houses at the site of the ancient city of Troy

The Aegean coast, which has a 5,000-year history of human occupation, is important from an archaeological viewpoint. The historical sites of Troy and Pergamum are here, as well as ancient Ionia to the south.

The Mediterranean region offers some of the most beautiful scenery in the entire country. It's little wonder that this is where many Turks head when vacation time rolls around. In the east are the imposing Taurus Mountains and rugged coastlines that once sheltered daring pirates.

Western Anatolia is covered with mountain ranges and is home to a series of long rivers including the Sakarya and the Menderes. The Turkish Lake District, an area of shallow lakes, is found between the peaks of the Taurus Mountains. This region stays chilly even in the summer.

Central Anatolia features a combination of hot, dry summers and snowy winters, as well as rolling hills and tiny villages. This is where Cappadocia is located. People

Chimney-like rock formations were used as homes and churches by the ancient peoples of the Cappadocia region.

The plains of Eastern Anatolia

have lived in this area for 8,000 years, and it has many archaeological records and sites. This region is considered to be Turkey's heartland because it is where the first Turkish tribes settled back in the tenth century.

Eastern Anatolia is vastly different from other parts of Turkey. It is far more isolated and underdeveloped. The land is barren, with severe weather during the short summers and long winters. Poverty is common here.

Southeastern Anatolia bends somewhat like a bow along the edges of the Tauras Mountains. It shares borders with Syria,

The City of Iskenderun

In the Hatay Province, located on a narrow section of land that reaches south in Turkey's southern plains region, is the city of Iskenderun. In this historical city, Alexander the Great and his army of 35,000 men conquered Persian emperor Darius the Great's army of 100,000 way back in 333 B.C. To celebrate, Alexander founded this city and named it Alexandretta after—who else?—himself. The city, now known as Iskenderun, has a population of more than 150,000 today. It is a busy commercial center and port with a fine harbor.

Iraq, and Iran, so there is a decidedly Middle Eastern flair to its culture. It contains mountains and inactive volcanoes and is more uneven than the western sections. Turks are in the minority in this area; most of the population is made up of Kurds and Arabs.

How's the Weather?

The weather in Turkey is so varied that almost anyone's preferences can be accommodated. While sunshine warms the beaches in one area, there may be snow just right for skiing in another.

Turkey can be divided into six climatic regions. The Marmara and Thrace regions are warm in the summer and mild in the winter. The Aegean and the Mediterranean regions usually have hot, dry summers with temperatures rising into the 90's Fahrenheit (above 32° Celsius) and short, mild winters. The region of the Black Sea has cooler summers and quite a bit of rainfall—up to an amazing 100 inches (254 centimeters) a year. In Central Anatolia there are large temperature differences between seasons—even between day and night. Springs are wet, summers are dry, and winter is cold with some snow. Eastern Anatolia has the most extreme weather. Winters are bitterly cold, with temperatures as low as 40° below 0 Fahrenheit (-40°C), and snow may cover the ground for up to four months at a time. Even the summers never warm up quite as much as in the other regions. Southeast Anatolia, on the other hand, is the hottest area, with summer highs into the low 100's F (more than 38°C) and usually one or more droughts (extended periods with no rain).

When the Earth Shakes

The early morning hours of August 17, 1999, were quiet in the western Turkish city of Izmit. The quiet was suddenly broken at 3:02 A.M., when Turkey's second-strongest recorded earthquake hit. Measuring 7.0 on the Richter scale, the terrifying quake lasted 45 seconds. In those seconds, it destroyed almost 300,000 homes and 40,000 businesses. More than 500,000 people were left homeless. Almost 20,000 people died, and more than three times that number were injured. Roads were cut off completely, communication became impossible, and an oil refinery went up in flames. The following months brought more than 1,300 aftershocks. On November 12, a nearby area was hit again with a stronger earthquake that measured 7.2 on the Richter scale. Almost 900 people died in this disaster; 5,000 were injured; and an additional 80,000 were left homeless.

On February 3, 2002, Turkey shook again when an earthquake measuring 6.2 hit the province of Afyon, southeast of Istanbul. It hit just after 9:00 A.M. The quake left villagers homeless along with 45 people dead and 170 injured. Aftershocks followed, some measuring as high as 5.3 on the Richter scale.

Unfortunately, Turkey is becoming well known for its earthquakes. It sits directly on a major fault zone and has experienced eight large quakes (measuring 7.0 or higher) in the last sixty years—eighty in the last century. The majority take place on the western branch of the 750-mile (1,207-km)-long Anatolian fault located in the eastern Marmara region. Despite this history, the government was completely unprepared for 1999's disaster and had to depend almost entirely on volunteers for most of the rescue efforts. The Turkish government's slow response for relief effort was heavily criticized all over the world.

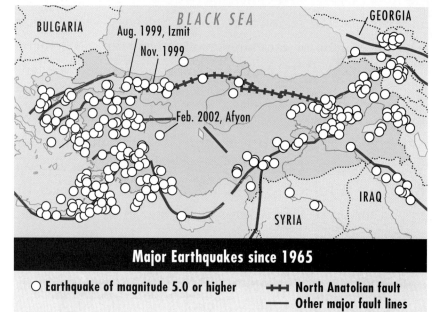

Major Earthquakes since 1965

○ Earthquake of magnitude 5.0 or higher   ┼┼┼ North Anatolian fault   — Other major fault lines

Turkey's Geographical Features

Largest City: Istanbul, 9.5 million people

Area: 297,614 square miles (770,760 sq km)

Coastline: 4,474 miles (7,200 km)

Largest Lake: Lake Van, 1,434 square miles (3,713 sq km)

Longest River: Kızıl Irmak, 842 miles (1,355 km)

Greatest Distance North to South: 465 miles (748 km)

Greatest Distance East to West: 1,015 miles (1,633 km)

Most Precipitation: Black Sea coastal region, 118 inches (300 cm) per year

Least Precipitation: Southeast Anatolia, 25 inches (64 cm) per year

Hottest Region: Southeast Anatolia, 115°F (46°C) in summer

Coolest Region: Eastern Anatolia, -40°F (-40°C)

Highest Point: Mount Ararat, 16,949 feet (5,166 m)

Turkey is a land that seems to offer something for everyone in terms of landscape, sites, climate, and style. Indeed, each summer over 10 million people travel to this unique land in search of warm seas, a hot sun, and lessons in ancient history. *"Hos geldiniz!"*—Welcome to Turkey!

Looking at Turkey's Cities

Antalya (above) is located on the southern coast of Turkey. Situated on a natural harbor, it is has long stretches of beautiful beaches that draw people from all over the world. While the population is usually around 1.5 million, that number swells by 300,000 to 500,000 during the summer season. Antalya is considered to be one of the most beautiful cities in Turkey. U.S. navy ships can often be seen docked in its bay.

Bursa, the fourth-largest city in Turkey with almost 2 million people, is located 145 miles (233 km) south of Istanbul. The city is dwarfed by Mount Ulu's 8,377-foot (2,553-m) peaks. Thought of as the heart of Turkish industry, Bursa is a mixture of modern factories and warehouses and historical landmarks. The *Yesil Camii*, or Green Mosque, and other examples of early Ottoman architecture are located here.

Bodrum (below) is situated on a peninsula. This town is the yachting center of Turkey. The area is famous for building a special kind of wooden-hulled yacht called a gullet. Its landmarks include the Castle of Saint Peter and the Bodrum Museum of Underwater Archaeology. Tourists from all over the world visit Bodrum during the summer months.

Edirne, which is called "The Gateway to Europe," is near the Bulgarian border. Its population is around 400,000. It has an interesting bazaar and is home to *Selimiye Camii*, the mosque that an architect named Sinan considered to be his masterpiece.

Istanbul (below), the biggest and best-known city in Turkey, is an incredible mixture of culture and religion. It is also the only city in the world that is located in two continents. Originally called Byzantium, its name was changed to Constantinople by Constantine I and then finally to Istanbul. The population of Istanbul is young; more than half of its 9 million people are less than twenty-five years old. Istanbul combines the most modern of buildings and businesses with some of the most impressive landmarks in the country, including the Blue Mosque, the Bosporus Bridge, the Hagia Sophia, and the Egyptian Spice Market.

Izmir is Turkey's third-largest city, with a population of almost 3.1 million. It is home to Turkey's second-largest port. Many of Izmir's most impressive historical buildings were destroyed in earthquakes and in a big fire in 1922. It was also the center of the destructive 1999 earthquake. Izmir is close to some famous historical sites, such as the ruins of Ephesus and Troy.

Fairy Chimneys and Drowned Cities

Cappadocia, in Central Anatolia, was once covered in molten lava and dust from the long-gone volcano of Mount Erciyes. The people who lived there carved their homes out of it. Cappadocia has more than 400 underground cities including one called Derinkuyu, which has an amazing eight levels, including stables, a school, churches, living quarters, and a dining hall. The area is covered in formations that have been called "fairy chimneys"—cone-shaped rocks that dot the landscape, rivaling the best scenery of science-fiction movies.

Aperlae is an island that lies about 90 minutes by boat from the city of Kas on the Mediterranean coastline. It has a pirates' cove and a fabulous underwater city. In the shallow waters, the outlines of streets and buildings are visible. The city sank below the surface of the water following an earthquake during the fourth century. On Kekova Island, the ruins of a church sit on the beach, and more ruins lie under the water.

In eastern Turkey is the valley of Harran, one of the oldest continuously inhabited places in the world. More than 2,000 people live there in beehive-like huts that date back to biblical times. The huts haven't changed a bit in all these years. They are still made of the one thing that is plentiful in the area—mud.

At one time, 20,000 people lived in the underground city of Derinkuyu.

The Flora and Fauna

Trees along the Black Sea mountains ablaze with color

T URKEY IS RICH WITH ANIMAL AND PLANT LIFE DUE TO A combination of factors. First, three seas surround the country. This helps to attract and cultivate various types of flora, or plant life, and fauna, animal life. Next, Turkey's industrial and agricultural development came late, allowing the plants and animals a chance to thrive without human interference. Add in the country's range of climates, and the environment is perfect for nurturing abundant life.

The Flora

This Middle Eastern country has more plant species than all of Europe put together. Turkey contains an incredible 10,000 kinds, a third of which grow only in Anatolia.

Trees and forests are abundant in Turkey. Along the Black Sea's mountain slopes, beech, oak, and maple trees thrive.

Opposite: **Trees bloom on the rocky shores of Lake Van**

The Flora and Fauna **35**

In the northwest region, sycamore, chestnut, and pine grow. The southwest offers oak, wild olive, and licorice trees. Much of the wood from these trees is exported, but it is also used for local building and furniture.

Wildflowers seem to be a specialty in this country. Many ornamental flowers, such as the crocus and the lily, are grown from the wild species found here. Turkish farmers grow and export many varieties of flowers, including snowdrops, snowflakes, and cyclamen.

In Praise of Tulips

The national flower of Turkey is the tulip. As early as A.D. 1000, records show that tulips were being grown in Turkey. In the thirteenth century, a Turkish poet named Rumi wrote praises of tulips in his poems. The reign of Sultan Ahmet II (1703–1730) was known as the Tulip Period. Ambassadors were sent to Europe to watch other cultures and to bring back new ideas, including planting tulips in home gardens to make them appear more elegant.

Turkish poppies

Farmers in the Isparta region in southwestern Anatolia are recognized worldwide for their roses. They grow these delicate and beautiful flowers here and then export their oil—called *attar* of roses—to France for use in making perfume. Other farmers grow crops of red Anatolian poppies, which they sell around the world for use in medical prescriptions. The Aegean and the Mediterranean areas are known for their lovely pink and white oleanders.

Turkey has a large number of national parks, many of which give visitors a chance to see an incredible array of flora. They offer quite a sight for the eyes, as well as scents for the nose.

Heading Out to the National Parks

The first national park in Turkey was established in 1958. Since then, the number of national and natural parks and forests has continued to grow.

Forty years ago, anyone who tried to visit Nemrut Mountain, a national park in the eastern part of Turkey, would have been in for quite a difficult trip. Located on the country's fifth-highest peak, at about 7,000 feet (2,100 m), Nemrut could only be reached on foot or by donkey. This meant at least a two-day trip. Thanks to a paved pathway today, however, travelers can get there by car or bus—unless it's between the first of October and the first of May, when the park is closed due to snow.

The trip is worth it—even with the ever-present chill. The park is a funeral monument to King Antiochus I, a rather vain ruler of the Commagene Kingdom in the first century B.C. At the summit, visitors are greeted by the regal heads of many gods and kings (right) that Antiochus had his workers carve and place facing the east and the west. Antiochus's own face is included, along with those of the Greek gods Apollo, Zeus, and Hercules, because Antiochus thought of himself as their equal. Each head is taller than the average man and seems to watch the world go by in silence.

Experts consider Nemrut Mountain to be a feat of engineering that compares to the ancient pyramids of

National Parks of Turkey

A Aladaglar	**J** Gelibolu Yarimada	**S** Kasdagi
B Altindere	**K** Göreme	**T** Kovada Gölü
C Baskomutan	**L** Gulluk Mountain	**U** Köprülü Canyon
D Belgrad Ormani	**M** Hailla Voisi	**V** Kus Cenneli (sanctuary)
E Olympus Beydaglari	**N** Honaz Mountain	**W** Nemrut Mountain
F Lake Beyşehir	**O** Ilgaz Mountain	**X** Ulu Mountain
G Birecik (sanctuary)	**P** Kackardaglari	**Y** Sipil Mountain
H Bogazkale Alacahoyuk	**Q** Kangol Sahara	**Z** Yedigoller
I Camlik	**R** Karatepe	

Egypt. No one knows how the workers were able to drag these incredibly heavy statues thousands of feet up the mountain without modern machinery.

Located outside the city of Antalya, Köprülü Canyon National Park is part of Selge Canyon, which extends to the Mediterranean coast. The landscape within the park is breathtaking, ranging from clear, white-capped waters to fairy chimneys and other rock formations. The ancient city of Selge, which still contains its original theater, is found there. The backdrop of the snow-capped peaks of the Kuyucuk Mountains was designed by nature.

The Olympus Beydaglari National Park is on the Mediterranean coast near Antalya. It features mountains 6,000 feet (1,829 m) tall, a wonderful beach, and ruins to explore. In the spring, the park truly comes alive as the lavender and roses bloom, attracting colorful butterflies. Another unique feature of this park is the shearwaters found there. These oceanic birds fly around the park in large flocks.

Unique to Turkey

Turkey has a number of animals that live nowhere else. They include a species of pheasant (above) called *Phasianus colchicus* and a type of wild sheep (right) called *Ovis musimon anatolica*. The Anatolia leopard is also found only in Turkey.

The Fauna

As many plant species as Turkey has to offer, their number is small in comparison to the number of animal species—more than 80,000! Some of the most common wild animals include wolves, foxes, boars, beavers, bears, deer, hyenas, and mountain goats. Typical domestic animals include water buffalo, camels, horses, donkeys, sheep, and cattle.

One type of animal that Turkey certainly has a lot of is birds—of all shapes, sizes, and colors. From vultures and eagles to flamingoes and sparrow hawks, birds visit Turkey from all over the world. Other birds that live or pass through here include crested larks, yellow black-headed buntings, bee-eaters, partridges, quail, and wild geese. Bird-watching is a sport that is growing in popularity with both residents and visitors, especially in spring and autumn, when the birds begin to migrate across the country.

Flamingoes are one of many types of birds found in Turkey.

The Birds' Crossroads

In the month of May, bird-watchers of all ages clean off their binoculars and get ready to see some incredible sights as migration season begins. Sultan Sazligi, a complex of freshwater marshes, salt lakes, and mud-flats just southeast of Cappadocia, is the crossroads of two migration routes.

In May it's easy to spot more than 300 different bird species flying overhead in numbers that mount up to more than 700,000! About a quarter of these birds stop and nest in the area. The two dozen wetlands found throughout Turkey provide shelter for more than 25,000 birds.

Turkey has several bird sanctuaries, including *Kus Cenneti* (Bird Paradise), by the Sea of Marmara, and Birecik, close to the Syrian border. They are home to some of the more common species, as well as some endangered ones.

Flight of the Storks

Twice a year, the skies over Istanbul are filled with the breathtaking sight and sound of migrating storks. The Bosporus Strait, a 22-mile (35-km)-long channel of water that divides the continents of Europe and Asia in Turkey, is part of their annual migration route. For several weeks each spring and fall, Istanbul's skies play host to more than a quarter of a million storks flying from one area of the world to another. Those who stay to breed build huge nests in minarets, on rooftops, and atop telephone poles.

The loggerhead turtle is an unusual animal that can be found in Turkey. Loggerhead turtles live in coastal bays and open seas of several parts of the world, including Turkey's Aegean coast. There, on Daylan Beach, is one of the world's biggest and most important nesting grounds for loggerheads. These lumbering, 3-foot (91-cm)-long creatures go to this beach to lay their eggs. Because of growing tourism, however, it is not necessarily a safe place for them to do so. The turtle's eggs are threatened because during their two-month gestation, the time they need to mature to the point of hatching, they are very vulnerable to being trampled on or dug up by vacationers. In addition, when the eggs hatch, the baby turtles are naturally attracted to the sight of reflected moonlight on the ocean surface. However, hotel lights can distract them and slow down their progress. This makes it easier for predators to grab them. Recently, Daylan Beach has been declared protected. It is still open to the public, but no building is allowed.

A loggerhead turtle works its way to the sea on Daylan Beach.

A Look at the Unusual

Among all the animals found in Turkey, some are quite unique and endangered. The bald ibis, for example, is close to being extinct. One of the world's two remaining nesting places for the bald ibis is located in the bird sanctuary near Urfa from mid-February to early July. The major wetlands within Turkey also provide shelter to endangered birds such as the Dalmatian pelican, the pygmy cormorant, and the slender-billed curlew, as well as to plants including buttercups, water mint, water lilies, and tamarisks.

In eastern Turkey is Lake Van, the country's largest inland body of water and one of the world's largest lakes. Living there are the mysterious and strange Van cats (below). These fluffy white creatures often have one blue eye and one green eye. Unlike domestic cats, they love to go swimming and often dive into the large lake just for the fun of it. Their species is endangered, but an organization called the Van Cat Research

Institute is helping to turn that around. A number of Turks keep Van cats as pets in their homes.

Around the mountainous town of Kangal lives a type of work dog that is bred specifically to protect flocks of livestock from hungry packs of wolves or bears that might be roaming the area. Called Anatolian Kangal dogs (above), these strong dogs would intimidate any animal. They reach about waist-high on the average adult and weigh up to 135 pounds (61 kilograms). Considered to be Turkey's national breed, these powerful dogs have come to the attention of breeders all over the world. They are very good-natured animals but are fiercely protective—as anyone who gets between them and their flocks will quickly find out. Some families in Turkey keep these dogs as pets. The government recently made it illegal to export the dogs without a license.

Along Turkey's Aegean and Mediterranean shores lives one of the world's ten most threatened animal species, the monk seal. Since the early 1970s, the number of these unique animals has dropped a shocking 80 percent due to a combination of water pollution, fishing nets, and being killed as pests. There are fewer than 300 monk seals left in the world, and about 50 of them live along Turkey's isolated coastlines.

The endangered monk seal

In 1993, the National Wildlife Federation and the Turkish Ministry for the Environment banded together to help these animals. The area that monk seals live in is now designated as "specially protected," and no diving, fishing, or boating is allowed near the breeding grounds. With luck, measures like this will help to get the monk seals off the endangered list.

Turkey is a rich country in many ways, and its incredibly diverse plants and animals are certainly one of them. They make it a more beautiful place, from the earth to the skies.

A 3,000-Year History

The Gate of Lions is the entrance to the capital city Hattusas, today known as Bogazkale.

ONE ELEMENT THAT MAKES TURKEY SUCH AN INTERESTING and unusual country is how far back its history reaches. Archaeologists have found evidence of advanced societies living in this part of the world as early as 6000 B.C. As in many countries of the world, the years saw shifting power as one empire after another took control, and then others came along to challenge it.

The Empire of the Hittites

The first group of people recorded as living in Turkey migrated to Central Anatolia from Europe and Central Asia. Called the Hittites, this extremely powerful line of people was almost unknown in history until a Frenchman named Charles Texier came across the ruins of their capital at Bogazkale in 1834.

Opposite: **Remains of Perge, an ancient, prosperous, Roman-ruled city**

These unearthed stone tablets describe the daily life of the Hittite people.

Later, excavations by German archaeologists unearthed 10,000 clay tablets that explained the Hittite history—once experts learned how to translate them.

The Hittites were the leading rulers of the Middle East in 1500 B.C. They focused on conquering much of Anatolia, parts of Mesopotamia, and Syria. They held control of this region for hundreds of years, until 550 B.C. Afterward, the Persian Empire took all of Anatolia and Thrace. The Persians remained until 331 B.C., when the arrival of 21-year-old Alexander the Great from Macedonia crushed their army. After Alexander died eight years later, many people fought over Anatolia.

Timeline of Dynasties

1550–550 B.C.	Hittite Empire
513–331 B.C.	Persian Empire
331–323 B.C.	Alexander the Great's Empire
63 B.C.–A.D. 330	Roman Empire
330–1071	Byzantine Empire
1071–1095	Seljuk Empire
1096–1243	Seljuk Empire (except for western third of Anatolia)
1243–1326	Mongolian Empire
1326–1453	Ottoman Empire (except for Constantinople)
1453–1923	Ottoman Empire

The Legend of Troy

Once thought to be just a legend handed down for generations through the stories of Homer's the *Iliad* and the *Odyssey* and the familiar tale of the Trojan Horse, the real city of Troy was rediscovered in the nineteenth century. It is near Çanakkale, in the northwestern part of Anatolia.

There were almost 3,000 years of continual settlement in Troy, which historians have divided into nine eras. The first was in 3000–2400 B.C., and the last ended in 334 B.C. This unique area has given scientists the chance to explore the cultural development of a single site over a huge period of time—a rare opportunity.

And yes, the Trojan Horse of many stories is indeed in Troy. It isn't the original one, however; instead, it is a model made from images found on coins and pottery excavated at the site.

For centuries, while small kingdoms would rise, they would fall just as quickly. This finally stopped in 63 B.C., when Roman general Pompey took the region. Anatolia was at peace as part of the Roman Empire for almost 400 years.

Shifting Power

In A.D. 330, the Roman emperor Constantine the Great came to Turkey and moved the capital from Rome to the Thrace town of Byzantium. He renamed it Constantinople after himself, and because Constantine was a Christian, his empire was, too.

The circus and hippodrome of Christian Constantinople

Sixty-five years later, the Roman Empire split into two sections. The western part, which included the Byzantine Empire, began to grow even stronger. It continued to thrive for centuries, until the mid-1000s. Then, a group of Seljuk Turks from central Asia battled the Byzantine army at the Battle of Malazgirt and won. Christianity was no longer observed. Islam became the empire's religion. The language also changed from Greek to Turkish.

In 1095, Christians from western Europe made Turkey part of their Crusades and attempted to drive out the Turks. They managed to win back about one-third of the country before they headed to other lands, but the Seljuks still controlled the remaining two-thirds. In 1243, a group of Asian nomads called Mongols invaded the area and won temporary control. However, due to internal problems, the Mongolian Empire fell apart by the early 1300s. Along came a new group that would begin the most powerful and long-lasting empire of all.

The Ottomans

During the 1300s, a group of Turks calling themselves Ottomans began creating a huge empire. In 1326, they seized Bursa, and by the end of the

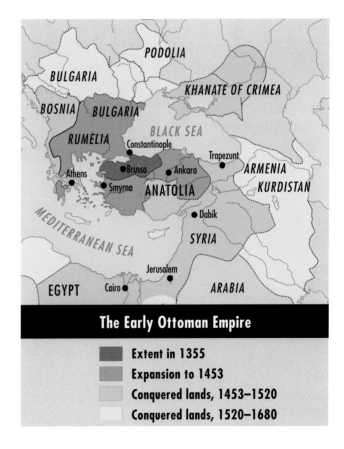

The Early Ottoman Empire

■ Extent in 1355
■ Expansion to 1453
□ Conquered lands, 1453–1520
□ Conquered lands, 1520–1680

A depiction of the 1453 attack on Constantinople by the Ottomans

century, they had control over the western two-thirds of Anatolia and most of Thrace. The only part left to the Byzantines was right around Constantinople. Under the leadership of Mehmet II, the Ottomans conquered that city in 1453, renamed it Istanbul, and made it their capital.

The rest of the 1400s and the 1500s saw the Ottoman Empire at its most powerful. It became the leading naval power in the entire Mediterranean region, and it conquered what is now Syria, Egypt, and Hungary, to name but a few areas. The Ottomans controlled all of the Balkans, all of the

Middle East (with the exception of a small portion of Saudi Arabia), and even parts of North Africa. Their expansion, which has rarely been equaled in history, encompassed more than 12.5 million square miles (32 million sq km). The Ottomans were not only determined, but also well organized. Unlike other conquerors, they restricted most of their fighting to the battlefield rather than taking it into the villages and towns, in the hopes of living with the people peacefully after their conquest.

Europeans began to worry that the Ottomans would target them next. Indeed, in the following years, European leaders found themselves having to defend their countries against these sultans. In 1529, European forces successfully defended Vienna. In 1571, the Spanish fleet defeated the Ottoman navy, and in 1683, it defeated another Ottoman attempt to capture Vienna. By the turn of the eighteenth century, the Ottoman Empire's

A Traveling Man

All he wanted to do his entire life was travel—and that is exactly what he did. Evliya bin Dervis Mehmet Zilli was born in 1611 in Istanbul. From his earliest days, he knew that he wanted to explore the world. His father was an artist who had served with many sultans in his lifetime. He was also a talented storyteller who filled his son's ears with endless adventure stories that fed the boy's passion to travel.

Zilli began by exploring every nook and cranny of his hometown until there wasn't a corner of it he didn't know or a person he hadn't spent time talking with.

Then, in 1640, he went to Bursa, followed by a sea voyage to Izmit. His journeys had just begun. For the next forty years, Zilli fought in battles, traveled by boat and foot, and even became the chief muezzin and accountant of Melek Ahmet Pasha, governor of the western regions of the Ottoman Empire. With Pasha, he explored all of Europe.

Zilli wrote about his explorations in a nearly 6,000-page book called *Book of Travels*. It is still read today and allows the armchair traveler to share in Zilli's undying passion to see foreign lands.

Mapmaker

It's a mystery that has yet to be solved. Piri Reis, an admiral in the Turkish fleet during the sixteenth century, loved to draw maps. Studying others' maps and then creating his own was his favorite thing to do. In the process, he created a mystery that scientists still have not been able to solve.

In 1513, Piri Reis drew a map of the world, based on what he had seen himself and what he had been told by other travelers. The original map wasn't found until hundreds of years later in 1929. It amazed cartographers, or mapmakers, around the world. The map showed the northern coast of Antarctica, which is incredible because Antarctica wasn't discovered until 1818, some 300 years later! To add to the mystery, his map also had correct longitudes for Antarctica, and they weren't discovered until the late 1770s. Piri Reis's maps are still considered to be some of the most amazing in the world.

domination was dwindling. Its attempts to conquer other lands were not working. In fact, the Ottomans were losing territories.

The Sick Man of Europe

As the eighteenth century gave way to the nineteenth, the Ottoman Empire, once considered one of the strongest empires of the world, was now nicknamed "The Sick Man of Europe." The Treaty of Adrianople in 1829 was more than the empire could recover from. In the treaty, Greece, Serbia, and Romania all received their long-desired independence, and Russia gained control of the Danube River. The following year, Turkey lost Algeria to France. By 1818, it also lost Tunisia to France, and Cyprus and Egypt to Great Britain.

The Ottomans tried to stop this decline by doing what governments still do today—making internal changes. They reorganized their military and focused on improving their educational systems. In 1876, they adopted their first-ever Constitution, which might have helped except their new ruler, Sultan Abdul Hamid II, threw it aside. Instead he ruled as an autocrat, with complete authority over everything. He used fear to rule. He made life in Turkey oppressive and difficult for everyone, including both Muslim Turks and the religious minorities. This led to anger and violence. Not too surprisingly, it also led to change.

Time for Changes

In the late 1890s, a small group of Turkish students and military personnel decided they could not tolerate Abdul Hamid II's

Young Turks enter Constantinople

actions. Calling themselves "Young Turks," they met in secret and made plans to stop him. In 1908, they led a revolt and forced Hamid II off the throne. His brother, Muhammad V, took over, but still Turkey lost more territories. By 1914, it had lost all of its European land except for Thrace.

In 1914, Turkey entered World War I (1914–1918) on Germany's side. When Allied troops tried to get control of the Bosporus and Dardanelles Straits in order to get aid to Russia, the Ottomans drove them back. Once the war was over, Great Britain, France, and the other Allies wanted to end the

Ottoman Empire, so they sent troops into Istanbul. In 1919, Greece landed its troops in Izmir and marched into central Turkey. The Turkish people grew more and more upset at the sultan's inability to defend their country. A new leader was needed, and one was ready—and waiting.

Father of the Turks

Already a military hero, Mustafa Kemal was anxious to help his country head in an all-new direction. He helped to organize a nationalist movement, whose members set up a new, temporary government in Sivas. In April 1920, the Turkish

Mustafa Kemal (fifth from left) with officials at the headquarters of the nationalist government in Angora

Grand National Assembly was formed and Kemal was elected its president. Later that year, on August 10, Sultan Mehmet VI was forced to sign the Treaty of Sèvres with the Allies, which guaranteed independence for some parts of the Ottoman Empire and gave other parts to the Allies. As the Turks' frustration with the sultan grew, their appreciation for Kemal and what he was trying to do also grew. Kemal's group drove the Greek troops out of Turkey, eliminated the sultan's office, and drew up a new peace treaty with the Allies. The Treaty of Lausanne, signed in 1923, set the boundaries of Turkey as they are today. The assembly declared Turkey a republic with Kemal as president. In 1934, Kemal was given the name *Atatürk*, "Father of the Turks."

The 1920s and 1930s were full of changes for Turkey. Atatürk made sweeping changes in every aspect of the country—from the educational system to the legal system, from what people wore to how they wrote their names. While some Turks revolted against these changes, most saw each one as a way to modernize and improve their country and felt that Atatürk was the leader they had been searching for. Although he died in 1938, his attitudes live on today as do his changes.

Transition to Democracy

When World War II (1939–1945) began, Turkey managed to stay out of it until 1945, when it entered on the side of the Allies. When the war was over, the Soviet Union wanted control of eastern Turkey so that it could build military bases along the Straits and control eastern Turkey's territory. Turkey turned to the West for help. In 1947, U.S. president Harry Truman issued the Truman Doctrine. It stated that the United States would provide help to any country, including Turkey, that was being threatened by *communism*, a system in which everything belongs to the government and is shared equally among the people. Turkey received millions of dollars in economic and military aid. In return, it allowed the United States to build and operate military bases in Turkey.

In 1946, Turkey's transition from a one-party state to a multiparty democracy went surprisingly smooth. This was partially due to the efforts of Ismet Inonu, Atatürk's successor, who oversaw his country through the transition.

In 1950, the Democratic Party won control of the Grand National Assembly for the first time. Things began to go downhill for Turkey. Exports were down, national debt was up, and there were more restrictions on the rights of the people. The press was not allowed to discuss these problems, and journalists who tried to do so were put in prison.

On May 27, 1960, military officers known as the National Unity Committee took control of the government and placed the political leaders on trial. Prime Minister Adnan Menderes was convicted and executed, and President Celal Boyar was given a sentence of life in prison. Boyar was later released, and a new Constitution was adopted.

The last several decades have continued to present challenges to this country. Turkey and Greece have continually fought over the strategically located Mediterranean island of Cyprus, where about 88,000 Turkish Cypriots and 24,000 immigrants now live. Finally, in 1974, when Greek military officers overthrew the president, Turkey sent more than 30,000 troops to the island and captured 40 percent of the territory. Cyprus remains two separate republics to this day, even though neither side is happy about it.

The 1970s saw a series of prime ministers come and go in Turkey, and its government remained unstable. There was another military coup in 1980, and in 1982, yet one more Constitution was created. Turkey returned to civilian rule the following year. The country continues to struggle with a great divide between nonreligious and religious groups within its society.

In 1990 and 1991, during the Persian Gulf War, the United States used Turkey as a staging base for air attacks on Iraq. The Turks helped the effort by shutting down Iraq's oil pipeline, which carried oil to the Mediterranean Sea, and allowed the United States to use their airfields. While some Turks objected to Turkey's involvement in this war, the president at the time, Turgut Ozal, hoped the country would be rewarded for its support. He also wanted to demonstrate to the rest of the world that Turkey could be counted on as a stable and dependable ally.

U.S. troops at a Turkish airbase during the Persian Gulf War

A Look Inside the Topkapi Palace and the Imperial Treasury

Located in Istanbul, the Topkapi Palace (above) was built in the fifteenth century and used by sultans and their families for more than four centuries. At one time, 50,000 people lived and worked there! It is the oldest and largest palace in the world. From the outside it looks much like a fort, with high walls surrounding all the buildings.

The Topkapi Palace is divided into three main areas: the *Birum*, or "Outer Palace," the *Enderum*, or "Inner Palace," and the *Harem*, or "Courtyards." At one time, it even had its very own zoo. The palace contains gardens, endless courtyards connected by gateways, and the oldest Byzantine church in the entire city.

The Imperial Treasury is found within Topkapi Palace. It holds such riches as the world rarely sees, including ivory book covers, slabs of emeralds, and the fifth-largest diamond in the world, weighing in at 84 carats.

The New Face of Government

TURKEY HAS HAD THE SAME BASIC STRUCTURE OF GOVERN-ment since the republic was declared in 1923. Its third and current Constitution was adopted in 1982. In Turkey's parliamentary form of government, there is a president, a prime minister, a cabinet, and a legislature called the Grand National Assembly. Turkey is the only predominantly Muslim country to remain committed to democracy for half a century.

In May 2000, Ahmet Necdet Sezer was elected by the Grand National Assembly. As president, he is commander in chief of the armed forces and the presiding officer at cabinet meetings. The prime minister is the leader of the political party with the most seats in Parliament. He or she is considered to be the head of the government. Bulent Ecevit became prime minister in 1999.

Opposite: **A bust of Mustafa Kemal, who led Turkey to independence**

Left: **Turkey's president, Ahmet Necdet Sezer**

Right: **Prime Minister Bulent Ecevit**

Grand National Assembly in session

The Turkish National Anthem

Adopted in 1921, the Turkish national anthem's lyrics were written by Mehmet Akif Ersoy (1873–1936). The music was written by Zeki Ungör (1880–1958).

"March of Independence"

Fear not and be not dismayed, this crimson flag will never fade.
It is the last hearth that is burning for my nation,
And we know for sure that it will never fail.
It is my nation's star, shining forever,
It is my nation's star and it is mine.

Frown not, fair crescent, for I am ready to die for you.
Smile now upon my heroic nation, leave this anger,
Lest the blood shed for thee be unblessed.
Freedom is the right of my nation who
Worships God and seeks what is right.

The cabinet is known as the Council of Ministers. Members of the cabinet are nominated by the prime minister and appointed by the president. They keep watch over the different governmental departments. The Grand National Assembly is elected by the people. Its 550 members are responsible for actions such as making laws, accepting treaties, and declaring war. If the president does not approve a bill that has been passed by the legislature, it will be returned to them. If the assembly approves it a second time, however, it becomes a law.

The voting age in Turkey is eighteen. Women have been allowed to vote since 1934, earlier than they could in many other Western democracies.

Judicial Power

The court system in Turkey handles commercial disputes, or cases between companies, as well as criminal trials. The Court of Cassations reviews the decisions of the lower courts, while the Constitutional Court is responsible for determining the legality of laws passed by the legislature. Judges are chosen by a Supreme Council of judges and prosecutors. They are in charge of determining if the laws the legislature passes are truly legal.

NATIONAL GOVERNMENT OF TURKEY

Executive Branch

| PRESIDENT | PRIME MINISTER |

COUNCIL OF MINISTERS

Legislative Branch

GRAND NATIONAL ASSEMBLY
(550 MEMBERS FOR FIVE-YEAR TERM)

Judicial Branch

| CONSTITUTIONAL COURT | COURT OF CASSATIONS/APPEALS |

The Crescent and the Star

The flag of Turkey, adopted in 1936, was designed with the traditional Islamic symbols of a white crescent moon and a five-pointed star on a red background. Red was used to represent the color of the Ottoman Empire. The national motto is *"Yurtta sulh, Cihanda Sulh,"* which means "Peace at home, Peace in the world."

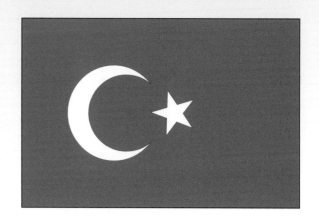

Local Government

Turkey is divided into eighty provinces, each with its own governor. Each of these provinces is further separated into counties, districts, municipalities (communities that have at least 10,000 people), and villages.

Which Party?

Turkish soldiers, guardians of the nation

There are several political parties within Turkey. The largest of them are the Democratic Left Party (center-left) and the center-right Motherland and True Path Parties. Next come the Nationalist Action Party and the Virtue Party, which is pro-Islamic.

There are 480,000 men in the armed forces in Turkey. (Service branches include the army, the navy, and the air force.) Only men between the ages of twenty and thirty-two are allowed into military service. They may be drafted for eighteen months.

Father of the Turks

Anyone who happens to be standing in Turkey on November 10 at 9:05 in the morning will notice something decidedly unusual. Everyone—from people on the sidewalks and drivers in the streets to people eating in restaurants and executives making presentations—stops what he or she is doing and stands silent for one minute. This is done to honor one of Turkey's—and the world's—most esteemed leaders, Mustafa Kemal, or Atatürk, the "Father of the Turks." He died on this date in 1938. He could be described as Turkey's version of George Washington.

Born in 1881, Atatürk was a leader who did more to change and improve his country than almost any person in history. In 1923, he founded the Turkish Republic and was quickly elected its first president, a job that he held until his death fifteen years later. In those years, he managed to change things within Turkey's social, political, legal, economic, and cultural life. He led his nation to full independence; ended the Ottoman dynasty, which had been in control for more than six centuries; rewrote the Constitution; outlawed polygamy (having more than one spouse); and gave women the right to vote. His changes were felt everywhere—from the language people spoke to the way they worshiped. Atatürk's image is seen all over Turkey, from portraits on the wall of every government building and most homes to statues in parks, and on most denominations of money.

One hundred years after his birth, at the "Atatürk Centennial," the U.S. White House issued a statement that said, "Mustafa Kemal was a great leader in times of war and peace." One of the quotes for which he is best known reflects this: "I look to the world with an open heart full of pure feelings and friendship."

Tansu Çiller

A woman of ambition, Tansu Çiller was Turkey's first female prime minister. Born in 1943 in Istanbul, Çiller's career in politics began in 1990 when she became the assistant to the chairman of the True Path Party, Suleyman Demirel. She served as prime minister from 1993 to 1995.

Turkey has been a member of the United Nations since 1945. It is an associate member of the European Union, an organization of European countries that are trade partners. It is a long-time member (since 1952) of the North Atlantic Treaty Organization (NATO).

Atatürk's Address to Turkish Youth

Following is a translation of one of Atatürk's most famous speeches. He addressed it to the youth of Turkey to encourage their patriotism and involvement.

Turkish Youth!

Your first duty is forever to preserve and to defend the Turkish Independence and the Turkish Republic.

This is the very foundation of your existence and your future. This foundation is your most precious treasure. In the future, too, there may be malevolent people at home and abroad who will wish to deprive you of this treasure. If some day you are compelled to defend your independence and your Republic, you must not tarry to weigh the possibilities and circumstances of the situation before taking up your duty. These possibilities and circumstances may turn out to be extremely unfavorable. The enemies conspiring against your independence and your Republic may have behind them a victory unprecedented in the annals of the world. It may be that, by violence and ruse, all the fortresses of your beloved fatherland may be captured, all its shipyards occupied, all its armies dispersed and every part of the country invaded. And sadder and graver than all these circumstances, those who hold power within the country may be in error, misguided, and may even be traitors. Furthermore, they may identify their personal interests with the political designs of the invaders. The country may be impoverished, ruined and exhausted.

Youth of Turkey's future, even in such circumstances it is your duty to save the Turkish Independence and Republic.

You will find the strength you need in your noble blood.

Ankara: Did You Know This?

Ankara is a city that has seen incredible growth in the last eighty years. While it was once a small town of 20,000, today it has more than 3.6 million people. Located in the north-central Anatolia region, Ankara was chosen as Turkey's capital in 1923 by Atatürk. He wanted a city that had no connection with the Ottomans and that was centrally located within the country.

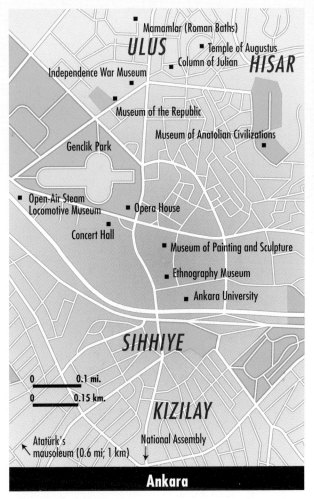

Ankara is a classic example of how Turkey is both modern and ancient. In the heart of the city is Kizilay, with high-rise buildings, shops, and an underground railway system. In other parts of the city are the hamman (Roman baths) and the *Anitkabir*, or mausoleum, of Atatürk. Indeed, Ankara is the place to go for museums. It is home to the Museum of Anatolian Civilization; the Independence War Museum; the Museum of the Republic; and the Ethnography Museum, for the study of specific cultures, to name a few.

CHAPTER

SIX

Shifting the Economy

EFORE ATATÜRK MOLDED TURKEY INTO ANOTHER COUNTRY, most of its economy was agriculturally based. The majority of the people lived on farms until the late 1920s. Then things changed. As Turks began to leave the villages for the cities, the economy began to shift.

More and more factories began to pop up. In 1923, there were just over 100 factories, and by 1941, there were more than 1,000. Today, Turkey has more than 30,000 factories that produce textiles, automobiles, lumber and paper products, and processed food. While most of these businesses were originally owned and controlled by the government, there has been a growing movement toward privately owned companies in recent years.

Opposite: **Major industrial factories contribute to the economic growth of Turkey.**

Almost half of Turkey's population works on farms. These workers sort corn.

Despite the growth of the factories, agriculture is still a driving force within the economy. Approximately 40 percent of the people still labor on farms, producing enough food for all the Turkish people as well as a surplus. This extra food is sold to other countries. The most fertile farms lie along the coasts, and fully half of

Farmers threshing wheat   them produce some kind of grain, including barley, corn, and wheat. Cotton is a big crop for Turkey, as is tobacco. Farmers harvest a variety of fruits, including melons, oranges, grapes, apples, and tomatoes, plus vegetables such as potatoes and sugar beets. Turkey produces various vegetable oils, such as olive and sunflower, for both commercial and domestic use. Some farmers also raise livestock, and their most valuable product is the wool from their sheep.

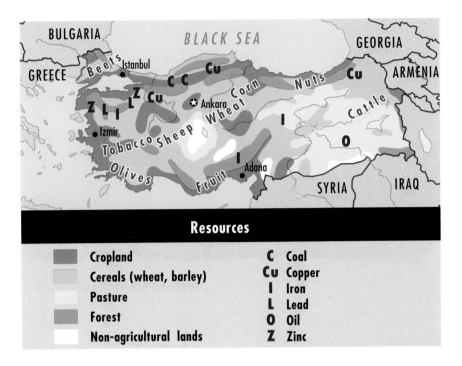

Resources

■ Cropland	**C** Coal
■ Cereals (wheat, barley)	**Cu** Copper
■ Pasture	**I** Iron
■ Forest	**L** Lead
■ Non-agricultural lands	**O** Oil
	Z Zinc

Women work in one of Turkey's many tobacco fields.

Tea and tobacco plantations are quite common throughout Turkey. This nation is responsible for growing about 3 percent of the world's entire tobacco supply, and about 40 percent of a specialized type called Oriental tobacco. In addition to this, Turkey is the sixth-largest producer of cotton and the world's largest producer and exporter of hazelnuts, used frequently in the making of coffee and chocolates.

Shifting the Economy **73**

What Turkey Grows, Makes, and Mines

Agriculture (2000)

Sugar beets	20,000,000 metric tons
Wheat	18,000,000 metric tons
Barley	6,800,000 metric tons

Manufacturing (1999)

Machinery	1.67 billion
Chemicals	279.8 million
Food and animals products	207.2 million

Mining (1999)

Copper	80,000 metric tons
Lead	12,000 metric tons
Zinc	5,000 metric tons

Oats and barley are common crops here. In fact, Turkey is classified as one of the four official gene centers for those grains by the National Wildlife Federation and other organizations. Other crops include chickpeas, lentils, almonds, figs, cherries, sour cherries, and apricots. Due to an increasing demand by the people, farmers also have started to grow tropical fruits such as kiwis, avocados, and bananas in the valleys and lowlands.

The Element of Mining

Turkey's soil is rich with a variety of minerals. There are over 4,000 different deposits in Turkey, and currently fifty-three different kinds of them are being commercially mined in the country. The primary one is copper. Although Turkey has several fairly large refineries, it does not have much oil.

Those Magic Carpets

Turkey is known all over the world for its carpets. Made in vibrant colors with striking patterns and shapes, these carpets appeal to people of many different ages, tastes, and backgrounds. Even the famous Italian traveler Marco Polo was recorded as commenting on their beauty when he passed through Anatolia in the thirteenth century.

While many carpets are sold to tourists, Turks use them for simple floor coverings, room curtains, covers for large cushions, or prayer rugs. Turkish carpet designs and styles are often handed down from mother to daughter.

The Grand Bazaar in Istanbul is considered one of the best places in the country to find a genuine Turkish carpet. There are also carpet centers in central Anatolia and the coastal regions. Shoppers in search of a special rug look for various things like how thick the weave is, how much silk and/or wool is in it, and what kinds of dyes were used.

The oldest Turkish carpets known of today were discovered in Konya early in the twentieth century. Woven more than 700 years ago, they are now on display in Istanbul. Historians believe that carpets date all the way back to the fourth century B.C. It was the Seljuks who supposedly made carpet weaving into an official business.

Today, a small number of women in Turkey still spend many long winter months weaving these beautiful rugs. The process begins with the wool. While most wool is mass-produced in factories, it is still possible to see a shepherd spinning raw wool while he tends his flocks. Dyeing is next. Originally, the dyes were made from natural products available at the time: leaves, bark, flowers, roots, and minerals. Now artificial dyes are also imported from nearby countries. Weavers can change the shade of the dye by adding ingredients such as yogurt, lemon juice, or salt to the mixture. The area of Göreme, in Cappadocia, has a training center that teaches people the ancient art of carpet weaving, and it is open to the public. The Dobag Project, in western Turkey, has also been established to show women how to use the traditional designs.

Shifting the Economy **75**

A Little Help from the Tourists

Turkey has made truly amazing progress in tourism, which is part of the service sector of the economy. People travel to and within this country to see its numerous sites and treasures. Not only does Turkey have ancient ruins and other historical places to visit, but it usually has as many as 150 archaeological digs going on at historic sites at any one time. Miles of beautiful coastline and seas bring vacationers from all over the world. Recently, there has been increasing interest in specialty types of travel, such as mountain climbing, whitewater rafting, fishing, and more. The government has responded to this interest by investing in the construction of hotels and restaurants and developing various travel packages.

In 1992, the number of foreign visitors to Turkey was almost 6 million, creating revenues of almost $3 billion. This number continues to rise. Turkey had more than 10 million visitors in 2000, with total revenues of almost $8 million.

Foreign Trade

Turkey exports goods and products to other countries, and it imports other goods and products from other countries. It trades primarily with Germany, and also with Italy, the United States, Russia, France, and the United Kingdom. Its main imports include chemicals, machinery, petroleum, iron, steel, and motor vehicles, while its main exports are clothing, textiles, cotton, fruits, nuts, wheat, and tobacco. In recent years, the country has spent more money on importing (about $56 billion) than it has received from exporting (about $27 billion), creating what is called an unfavorable balance of trade. This has hurt Turkey's economy. The 1999 earthquakes also

A freighter in port, heavy with imports, awaits unloading

The Turkish Lira

One Turkish lira isn't worth much these days: U.S.$1 equals 1.5 million Turkish lira. In fact, a simple breakfast may cost as much as 1 million lira! Bronze-, silver-, and gold-colored coins are available in denominations of 25,000, 50,000, and 100,000, and bank notes come in denominations of 5 million, 10 million, and 20 million. Atatürk's face graces the front of the bills, with a variety of historical sites throughout Turkey on the backside.

deeply damaged the economy because a good percentage of successful companies were destroyed in the event. Together, these elements have made Turkey's money, the lira, worth very little today.

Weights and Measures

Turkey uses the metric system of weights and measures.

$$\textit{The Tax Situation}$$

Another element that influences the condition of Turkey's economy, like any nation's economy, is the collection of taxes from its people. More Turks avoid paying income taxes than do pay them, primarily because many tax evaders are self-employed. There is no system to keep track of how much money self-employed people earn or whether they have paid their tax debt. It is often the lowest-paid people who pay, while the wealthier citizens manage not to. This creates tension among the people.

Mass transit is widely used throughout Turkey.

Turkey's Transportation System

Despite the continuing modernization of Turkey, only about 25 percent of its 238,000 miles (383,000 km) of roads are actually paved. Because fewer than 2 percent of its residents own their own cars, this isn't a huge problem. The majority of people use public transportation to get from one area or another. The bus system is inexpensive, but the buses are often crowded. Turkey has many different bus lines running across the country. Other people may choose to take taxis or trains.

Group taxis, called *Dolmus*, travel through some of the larger cities on set schedules. They range from a large car to a van or minibus. They are more convenient than a public bus and cheaper than a taxi, but they are usually tightly packed, especially during rush hour.

Turkey presently has 2 heliports and 121 airports. International flights land at and depart from Turkey in Istanbul, Ankara, Izmir, Antalya, Adana, Trabzon, Bodrum, and Dalaman airports. Because Turkey has so much seacoast, people also travel by boat. Turkish Maritime Lines operates car ferries from Venice, Italy, to Izmir once a week, and other ferry systems operate daily.

Danger on the Road

In spite of the limited number of cars on the road, Turkey still has a relatively high accident rate—thanks to narrow, curving roads, bumpy surfaces, and potholes. Animals are known to wander into the road now and then. Many motorcycle riders and farmers driving massive farm equipment don't turn their lights on at all, or they wait until they see another vehicle heading their way. Then they flash their lights on quickly, startling oncoming drivers. The police are beginning to hand out more tickets and fines for traffic errors in an attempt to bring more order and safety to the roads.

The Richness
of the People

The people of Turkey have changed along with their country. Their beginnings were primarily in Asia. About 85 percent of Turks are descended from people who migrated to Anatolia from central Asia during the A.D. 900s.

The first official census of Turkey was taken in 1927, when the population was about 13.5 million. Today, there are about 66 million Turkish people, and experts predict that by 2030

Opposite: **Although Turkey continues to grow as a modern country, the culture of its people is not lost.**

The growing population of Turkey fills this Ankara street.

The Richness of the People **81**

A School Ritual

Every morning in school, the students stand and recite a patriotic and dedicated message, which tells much about their character:

I am a Turk.

I am correct and hard working.

I am ready to sacrifice my existence for the existence of Turkey.

the population will be close to 85 million. As their numbers grow, the people are changing. However, they still honor many of their age-old traditions and values.

Turks are very hospitable people. A stranger at their door is considered a gift from God, and so he or she is welcomed and made to feel at home immediately. Turks also tend to be patriotic, generous, and competitive.

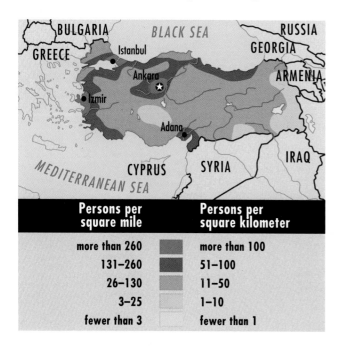

Persons per square mile		Persons per square kilometer
more than 260		more than 100
131–260		51–100
26–130		11–50
3–25		1–10
fewer than 3		fewer than 1

Where Turks Live

About 70 percent of the Turkish people live in the country's cities and towns, while the other 30 percent are in rural areas. It was not always like this. In the 1950s, in fact, it was the opposite, with more than 75 percent of the population living in villages and farms. As their country began to modernize, however, farmers and villagers were lured away from the rural areas by the cities' promise of more work and better education and

Population of Major Cities

Istanbul	9,057,747
Ankara	3,631,612
Izmir	3,066,902
Bursa	1,946,327
Konya	1,943,757
Adana	1,689,155
Antalya	1,477,347

A view of a housing area in Istanbul

healthcare. So many people decided to move that a lack of jobs and housing soon developed. The people were forced to look elsewhere. Quite a few Turks left their country for jobs

Opposite: **Kurdish woman
and children**

in other countries, including Germany, Austria, Canada, France, the Netherlands, and even Australia.

There is plenty of land in Turkey for the number of people who live there. The problem is, they all want to live in the same places! About half the population of Turkey lives on less than a quarter of the country's land. The most-populated areas are the narrow coastal belt that stretches from Zonguldak to Istanbul, around the Sea of Marmara and south to Izmir, and the Mediterranean Coast. Central and Eastern Anatolia, on the other hand, have very small populations.

Turkey's Minorities

The largest minority group in Turkey is the Kurds. Today, there are about 10 to 12 million Kurds in the country. They live in the mountainous region of the southeast as well as in the west, thanks to ongoing migration. This group is divided within itself, as the Kurds speak two main dialects, or varieties, of the Kurdish language. Many Kurds would like to form their own state, separate from Turkey, and this issue has come into direct conflict with Turkey's plans for future development. It is an ongoing battle that has yet to be solved. It has resulted in many incidents of violence.

A small portion of the Turkish population consists of Arabs, Armenians, and Greeks. Many are farmers who live near the Syrian border in Hatay, while some live in and around Istanbul.

Grammar, Grammar

While the Turkish language is considered difficult to learn, it helps that each letter is almost always pronounced the same way (unlike English). The most challenging letter is c, which is pronounced like an English j. For example, the word camii, which means "mosque," is pronounced JAH-mi. The Turks have an i without a dot. Without a dot, it is pronounced like "er" in English. The most confusing part of the language might be that suffixes are added to the root of a word to change its meaning. For example, bayrak means "flag," bayraktar means "flag bearer," and bayraktaroglu means "son of a flag bearer."

Speaking the Language

Over 85 percent of Turkey's citizens speak Turkish, and another 12 percent speak Kurdish. The rest speak Arabic, Greek, and other languages. No language other than Turkish is recognized or taught in the schools.

The Turkish language has a number of words in it with Arabic and Persian origins, despite Atatürk's determined efforts to get rid of them in the early 1920s. Atatürk directed a switchover in 1928 from the former Arabic alphabet to the 29-letter Latin alphabet used today. This was no easy chore!

Turkish Proverbs

A kind word warms a man throughout three winters.

Activity breeds prosperity.

Better a calf of one's own than a jointly owned cow.

God has created us brothers but has given us separate purses.

If you are an anvil, be patient; if you are a hammer, be strong.

Listen a hundred times; ponder a thousand times; speak once.

Wish well, be well.

With patience, mulberry leaves become satin.

Work as if you were to live forever; lie as if you were to die tomorrow.

OUR TAXI-BOATS ARE AT YOUR SERVICE
BOSPHORUS-EMIRGAN-KANLICA-SARIYER-R.KAVAĞI
PRİNCE ISLADS-KINALI-HEYBELİ-BÜYÜKADA
GOLDEN HORN-EYÜP

BOSHPHORE L'İLES DE PRİNCE İSLANDS
GORNE D'OR - EYÜP

BOSXPORUS PRİNZEN INSELN
GOLDENES HORN - EYÜP

Capitan Information

The Turkish Linguistic Association estimated that it would take six years to change the language over completely. Atatürk didn't agree. Instead, he told them that they had a mere six months to do it. They managed it, but barely. The Turkish Linguistic Association continues to try and create new words with Turkish-language roots, but the job is a challenging one.

A sign advertising taxi boat service in English as well as Turkish

Turkish Words and Phrases

Merhaba.	Hello.	Hayir	No
Gunaydin.	Good morning.	Lütfen	Please
Iyi geceler.	Good night.	Affedersiniz.	Excuse me.
Nasilsiniz?	How are you?	Turkce bilmiyorum.	I don't speak Turkish.
Tesekkurederim.	Thank you.	Anlamiyorum.	I don't understand.
Allahaismarladik.	Goodbye.	Nerede?	Where is it?
Evet	Yes	Saatiniz var mi?	What time is it?

The Ways of a Spiritual Life

To live in Turkey is to have a spiritual life. While there is no state religion and people have the freedom to choose, almost everyone who lives in Turkey is a Muslim—a follower of Islam. Yet many historical experts consider Turkey the cradle of Christianity. This is the country where the followers of Jesus Christ were first called "Christians" and where Noah's Ark is thought to have landed—on Mount Ararat, in eastern Turkey.

Opposite: **The remains of a Christian church serve as a reminder of Turkey's beginnings as the "cradle of Christianity."**

Constantine I the Great

It's little wonder that the Roman emperor known as Constantine went by the name of Constantine I: the Great. His official name was Flavius Valerius Aurelius Constantinus. The first emperor of Rome to become a Christian, he was born in A.D. 275 and died in A.D. 337. While he was in power, Christians in the region that is now Turkey once again had freedom to worship, and the Christian church was legalized. Property that had been taken from the Christians was returned.

Constantine rebuilt Byzantium, renamed it Constantinople, and made it the capital. Today that city is called Istanbul. Constantine built the first great Christian cathedral, along with other churches near Rome and in Turkey. When Constantine died, his empire was passed on to his sons, Constantius, Constans, and Constantine II.

Religions of Turkey

Muslim	98%
Armenian Apostolic, Greek Orthodox, Roman Catholic, Eastern Catholic, and Jewish	2%

For 2,000 years, Romans fought Christianity, and Christians escaped to Central Anatolia's Cappadocia. It wasn't until Constantine I embraced Christianity that this religious persecution stopped. For more than 1,000 years, Christianity was the main religion of the region, until the time of the Ottomans. In the 1920s, Atatürk declared that religious choice was a private decision. Many Turks objected.

The Five Pillars

The Islamic faith's main tenet, or belief, is submission—giving completely in to God. This began when the prophet Muhammad recorded the divine, or holy, revelations that he believed came from Allah (God). The revelations' 114 chapters and 6,236 verses make up the Qur'an. Muslims use the Qur'an

The Qur'an

as the basis for everything from their legal and judicial systems to their economic, political, and personal lives.

The Five Pillars of Islam dictate the following beliefs:

1. "There is no god but Allah, and Muhammad is his Prophet." Muhammad, along with Jesus, Adam, Noah, and Moses, were simply human messengers sent by Allah to spread the word of Islam to the world.

2. Muslims are to pray in the direction of Mecca, an important religious place where many people go to pray in Saudi Arabia. They are called to prayer five times a day, and they wash their hands, feet, and face before each prayer.

3. Muslims are to give generously to the poor, either directly or through their mosque. This money goes to the needy, thereby purifying it.

4. During Ramadan, the ninth month of the Muslim lunar year, believers fast (do not eat or drink) from before sunrise until after sundown.

5. Muslims who can afford it should travel to Mecca at least once in their lifetime. This pilgrimage is called the *hajj*. While many do complete the hajj, many others cannot afford it.

The Prophet Muhammad

Muhammad was an Arab who was born in Mecca in A.D. 570 and lived until A.D. 632. He lived as a trader and had a reputation for honesty and kindness. When he was forty years old, as the story goes, the angel Gabriel appeared to him. Gabriel let him know that he had been chosen to be a messenger of God, his prophet. For the next twenty years, Muhammad spread the word of Allah to all that he could reach, with rules of how they should lead their lives. When he died without naming a successor, Islam became divided.

A devout Muslim reads the Qur'an

Muslims make the tenets of the Qur'an part of how they live on a daily basis. They also use the guidelines put forth in the *Sunna*, a collection of stories, traditions, and sayings that Muhammad either said or modeled with his life. Muslims are taught to respect their parents, to be faithful to their spouses,

A Tour of the Green Mosque and the Green Tomb

It's hard to miss the Yesil Camii, or "Green Mosque," (below) in the city of Bursa. Built in 1419 by Mehmet I (who reigned 1413–1421), an early Ottoman sultan, it is an awesome sight. Its dome rises high above all of the surrounding buildings. Delicate carvings and turquoise, green, white, and blue tiles are spread throughout it in a variety of designs, from geometric patterns to circles and stars. An inscription inside states in Persian that the tiles are the work of the expert craftsmen of Tabriz (located in present-day Iran). The outside is almost entirely made out of marble.

Nearby is the *Yesil Turbe*, or "Green Tomb." Also built in 1419 and covered with green tiles, it is considered to be one of the most beautiful buildings in all of Bursa. The onion-shaped minaret caps and brick-and-stone exterior are nothing compared to the interior. The ornately decorated sarcophagus, or stone coffin (above), in it belonged to Mehmet I. It is empty because Muslim law forbids burial above the ground.

and to perform good deeds for others in their communities. The Islamic faith helped to promote equality among the people as well as the importance of virtue and charity. However, there is a great deal of argument in Turkey today about just how much influence Islam should have on people's lifestyles. Should Turkish society be worldly, or should it be religiously guided?

While some of Turkey's citizens are secular, being worldly rather than spiritual, the trend has been more to embrace religion than turn from it. However, Turkey is the only predominantly Muslim country to persist in being a part of the West through its memberships in NATO, its pro-Western foreign policy, and its close ties with the United States.

Further Divisions

Within Islam, there are several divisions, which have sometimes led to grief and frustration for all. When Muhammad died at the height of his power in 632, a caliph, or successor, had not been chosen yet. His followers were divided on who that person should be: Ali, Muhammad's cousin, or Abu Bakr, his father-in-law. Those who chose Ali are called Shiite Muslims, while those who preferred Abu Bakr are called Sunni Muslims. While the majority of the Muslims in Turkey today are Sunni, a rather liberal Shiite sect of about 20 million people called Alevis also lives there.

Another Muslim minority is the Sufis. Sufis hope to get closer to Allah by entering a trance state, which is a little like daydreaming. To do this, they use dance, music, and fire. It is from this sect that Turkey's famous "whirling dervishes"

developed. Although Atatürk shut down this branch of Islam, a group is still active today. These followers of the poet Mevlana Celaleddin-i Rumi are known as Mevlevi Sufis. Once a year, in December, the Mevlana Festival is held in Konya, and many tourists come to watch. The dervishes wear full-length, flowing white gowns and cone-shaped hats. To the sounds of drums and mystical music, they begin to whirl, and they continue whirling for hours. This dance symbolizes their union with Allah. Recently a group of Mevlevis called *Galata Mevlevihane* accepted women into their religious dancing ritual.

Whirling dervishes twirl for hours to become closer to Allah.

The Words of Rumi

Mevlana Celaleddin-i Rumi was a Turkish poet and philosopher in the thirteenth century. His ideas of brotherhood and understanding helped to establish the Mevlevi Sufi religious order. It accepts all religions as one and is founded upon the concepts of universal, unconditional forgiveness. Though Rumi lived more than 700 years ago, his birthday is still celebrated in Turkey every December. He felt that people need to be tolerant and patient, and this attitude is reflected in his words:

Come, come, come again, whoever you may be
Come again even though you may be a pagan or a fire worshipper
Our center is not one of despair
Come again, even if you may have
Violated your vows a hundred times, come again.

The Expanding World of Turkish Culture

THE PEOPLE OF TURKEY ENJOY HAVING FUN JUST AS MUCH as anyone else. The most popular types of recreation are family outings or meeting friends for tea and a game of backgammon at the nearest coffeehouse. Other times, Turks opt to play *okey*, a card game much like gin rummy only played with tiles.

Opposite: **A Turkish family gathers for an outing**

Turkish men playing a game of okey

A Turkish soccer fan supports his team by painting his face with the team colors.

Grab That Ball!

Turks like sports—especially soccer, or *futbol*. Four Turkish soccer teams have gained national status: Fenerbahce, Besiktas, Galatasaray, and Trabzon Spor. People get so passionate at some of these matches that the games are constantly patrolled by police watching for trouble. It isn't unusual to have a water cannon, armored vehicles, and an ambulance standing by for crowd control.

Other popular sports played in Turkey include archery, wrestling, and basketball. Swimming and sailing are well liked, as is golf, which attracts wealthy tourists. There are eight golf courses in the country and more than a dozen more under construction. *Cirit oyunu* is a fun sport to watch. It is similar to polo, except in this game, riders on horseback toss javelins at each other.

This rider prepares to toss his javelin during a match of cirit oyunu.

Oil 'Em Up!

Anyone looking for a little fun in Turkey in the summertime can watch a unique game called *yagli gures*, or greased wrestling.

The rules are similar to regular wrestling: A wrestler loses when his shoulder is forced to the ground or he gives up. In yagli gures, however, there is one definite difference: contestants put on a pair of leather pants and then cover their entire bodies with olive oil. Trying to pin someone who is that slippery makes the game much more challenging.

This type of game is thought to have begun in 1360 as a way to train soldiers to stay fit and quick. Today, it is one of Turkey's favorite summer sports. In late June or early July, at the Kirkpinar Festival near Edirne, more than 1,000 boys and men compete in four divisions: young boys, mid-height, full-height, and complete-height. Referees keep watch, and the average match lasts about thirty minutes, although they have been known to go on for as long as three hours. The winner is the last man standing—or sliding.

Pocket Hercules

His name is Naim Suleymanoglu but he's lovingly called the "Pocket Hercules." Because he is only 4 feet 11 inches (1.5 m) tall and weighs in at a little less than 140 pounds (64 kg), it's hard to imagine this man winning an Olympic gold medal in weightlifting—let alone three of them. That is exactly what he has done, though. Naim has made his country incredibly proud by taking home gold medals in the 1988, 1992, and 1996 Olympics Games. He even set a new world's record by lifting an unbelievable combination weight of 738.5 pounds (335 kg)—more than five times his own body weight!

Deve guresi, or camel wrestling, is another unusual Turkish sport. It pits two adult male camels against each other. An annual camel-wrestling festival is held in Selçuk in January, and other matches are held in the Aydin region during the winter months.

Skiing attracts many people to Turkey because more than half of it lies at an elevation of 3,000 feet (914 m) or higher and is frequently snow-covered. There are more than two dozen ski resorts scattered across the country, with the largest ones near Bursa and Erzurum. Interest in the sports of walking and mountaineering is spreading across Turkey, as is enthusiasm for some water sports, such as diving and waterskiing.

Turkish minstrels play traditional instruments

Here's Your Ticket

Istanbul hosts the International Music and Arts Festival in April, the European Jazz Days and the International Theatre Festival in May, and the International Music and Dance Festival in June. Turks have a deep appreciation of music, dance, and theater of all kinds. From opera to folk music, and from plays to concerts, the arts can be found in Turkey.

Music styles range all over the spectrum in this country. There's *sanaat*, sung in the original eighteenth-century style, as well as *ozgun*, which is protest music, usually centered on politics. Tarkan is one of Turkey's most popular pop singers, along with Kenan Dogulu, Sezen Aksu, and Sertap Erener.

Tarkan World

Called the Ricky Martin of the East, the Prince of the Bosporus, or the Turkish Michael Jackson, Tarkan Tevetoglu—or just plain Tarkan—is a singer who has created a sensation in Turkey and other countries around the world. He has released almost a half-dozen CDs and is considered to be one of the world's first non-English and non-Spanish musical megastars. Born in Germany, he lived in Turkey during his high school years and currently resides in New York. Tarkan writes most of his own songs, which he performs mostly in Turkish. He includes pop tunes, love ballads, and folk songs in his performances.

One of Tarkan's favorite singers is Sezen Aksu, who is called the Queen of Turkish Pop. Raised in Izmir, Aksu began her career in 1975 and had her first hit in 1978. She is also an actress and composes songs for other singers throughout Turkey.

Belly dancers perform
at nightclubs.

Folk music is performed at local festivals, and in Central
Anatolia, traveling singers, or minstrels, perform on a *saz*, a
lute-like instrument with three sets of strings.

In Turkey, common types of dancing include belly dancing
in cabaret shows and ballet at Istanbul's State Opera. Styles
range across the spectrum, however, evidenced by the fact

The Amphitheater

The city of Selçuk is located on the west coast of Turkey. One of its biggest attractions is an ancient amphitheater that can seat an incredible 25,000 people. Despite its age, it is still used for concerts today!

that a large outdoor disco is located in Bodrum and Ankara has its own ballet school.

Movies are also popular in Turkey. The featured shows are usually Hollywood blockbusters or other foreign films. Billboards outside the theater let people know what is currently playing, and show times are announced in the nation's largest newspapers, much as they are in the United States and Canada. Most movies have Turkish subtitles, but some are dubbed into Turkish.

Muhsin Ertugrul

Turkish cinema was just beginning when stage actor and director Muhsin Ertugrul began his career in 1922. The very first film ever made in Turkey was in 1914. It was a documentary produced for the army just as World War I was beginning. Ertugrul had been directing films in Germany since 1916. He came to Turkey to set up his own private company, called Kemal Film.

Ertugrul released two minor films in 1922, and then, in 1923, he released a movie called *Atesten Gomlek* (*The Shirt of Fire*). It was about Turkey's War of Independence. Shocking for its times, the movie featured two Turkish Muslim female actresses.

Ertugrul went on to direct *Bir Millet Uyaniyor* (*A Nation Awakes*) in 1932, still considered today to be one of Turkey's most important films. In 1934, his film *Leblebici Horhor Aga* won the first international award for a Turkish film at the second Vienna International Film Festival. By 1939, he had made more than twenty movies.

During his career in film, Ertugrul's diversity allowed him to be an actor, director, instructor, and critic. He is considered to be one of Turkey's most influential people in their history of cinema. During his seventy-year career he contributed to the Turkish cinema a wealth of knowledge, faith, and perseverance.

The Art of the Craft

Turkey has a long history of creating many kinds of arts and crafts. Turkey is also recognized worldwide for its unique architecture. Some of the most beautiful buildings in the

Turkish architecture has been an inspiration for buildings throughout the world.

Sinan and the Hagia Sophia

Born in Anatolia in 1489, Mimar Koca Sinan is considered to be the greatest architect of the Ottoman Empire. He was in charge of designing and building over 300 structures in Istanbul alone. Between 1538 and 1588, he created incredible masterpieces and lent his talents to everything from mosques, fountains, and palaces to chapels, tombs, harems, and hospitals.

One of Sinan's greatest achievements can be found in his renovation of Istanbul's Hagia Sophia (pictured), or *Aya Sova*—"the Church of Holy Wisdom." A Turkish historical tale tells how thousands of candles used to be lit inside, and their bright flames would reflect off of the marble walls so strongly that the building was used as a lighthouse. Whether that is true or not, the Hagia Sophia is considered a world landmark. It was designed by two mathematicians, Anthenius of Tralles and Isidorus of Meletus, and it took six years to build. Dedicated in 536, the building has already been through an earthquake, which sent its dome crashing to the floor, as well as destruction by thirteenth-century Catholic soldiers.

The church is huge, measuring 183 feet (56 m) high and 105 feet (32 m) on all four sides. Sinan added four towers under Mehmet II's orders. In 1932, Atatürk declared the Hagia Sophia a museum. Turks still debate today whether the building should be turned back into a church or kept open as a museum for tourists to visit. For now, tourists continue to walk through to see the stained-glass windows and religious mosaics. They can even walk to the marble square where Byzantine emperors were once crowned and see the library of Sultan Mahmut I, built in the 1730s.

world can be found in this country, and their styles of minarets and domes have inspired countless architects around the globe.

Craft work in Turkey goes back for centuries. The age-old traditions of painted miniatures, woven rugs, filigree (adding thin strands of silver and gold to various items), stained-glass production, and wood engraving continue today. Turks are also known for their excellent ceramics, from bowls to tiles.

Turkish ceramic bowls on display

Because the Qu'ran has restrictions on using the human form in art, many of the Islamic arts are done in geometric patterns with rich color and balance. The skill of calligraphy has been handed down for generations, and many otherwise common papers were turned into works of art as the words were drawn so beautifully. *Ebru*, the art of marbling paper, is still a popular craft. It was first developed in the fifteenth century. Embroidery is a skill that has been used throughout Turkey's history on everything from towels to tents, and from saddles to silk shirts.

Painting is an art form that got its start quite late in Turkey. It wasn't until the nineteenth century that Osman Hamdi Bey, an artist, founded the Academy of Fine Arts in Turkey. Through this academy, Turks were sent to Italy and France in order to learn painting skills from some of Europe's masters.

Orhan Pamuk, Turkey's most famous novelist

Turning the Page

Early Turkish literature was primarily poetry, oral history, and books about religion and life during the Ottoman times. Later, authors began to write about issues such as social justice, nationalism, and folk history. Speaking out against their nation's laws and philosophies frequently landed writers in prison or exile. Orhan Pamuk is Turkey's best-selling novelist. He is known internationally.

Three Popular Turkish Writers

Born in 1915, Aziz Nesin is one of Turkey's most popular writers. He was put in jail several times for his outspoken writings. He also won many awards, including the Golden Palm International Humorous Short Story Award in Italy, and the Asian and African Writers Union Lotus Award in the Philippines. In 1972, he established the Nesin Foundation, which helps to educate and care for homeless children. He died in 1995, but his short stories and novels continue to be read today.

Fuzuli, on the other hand, is one of Turkey's most famous poets. Born in 1495, he wrote poems using the three languages he knew well: Arabic, Persian, and Turkish. This made the poems very difficult to translate. In one of his best-known poems, "Ghazal," he wrote of the pain of losing someone he loved:

> Do not ask the morning wind how I felt
> When I was thinking of you, suffering,
> I burned out like a candle.
> As those who were with me
> On the night of separation

A man who is considered one of the most important figures in twentieth-century Turkish literature is Nazim Hikmet (1902–1963). Although his poems were translated into several languages, Hikmet was repeatedly arrested in Turkey for his political beliefs. He began writing at age fourteen, and as an adult he spent more than twelve years in prison for his words of social criticism. Despite this, he held a deep love for his country, as his poem "Memleketimi seviyorum" clearly states:

> I love my country. . .
> I love my country. . .
> I swung in its lofty trees, I lay in its prison.
> Nothing relieves my depression
> Like the songs and tobacco of my country. . .
> and them my working, honest, brave people.
> Ready to accept with the joy of a wondering child,
> Everything,
> Progressive, lovely, good,
> Half hungry, half full.
> Half slave.
> I love my country.

Turks enjoy a good chuckle just as much as people in other cultures. One common source of a few laughs is in stories about Nasreddin Hoca, a wise man who is supposed to have lived in Aksehir in the thirteenth century. Many jokes and folk tales are told about this character and his witty advice to others. For instance, "One day Nasreddin Hoca's friends asked him: 'At a funeral, where should one stand? Should it be in front of, beside, or behind the coffin?' 'Anywhere,' Hoca

Statue of the Turkish folkloric figure Nasreddin Hoca

replied, 'just not inside the coffin itself.'" Or, "One day, Hoca lost his donkey. While looking for it, he prayed and thanked God. 'Why are you so grateful when you have lost your precious donkey?' he was asked. 'I'm happy because I was not riding the animal at the time,' he replied. 'Otherwise, I would have been lost too!'"

Meeting Black-Eye

His shadow is reflected on the stage, and already people in the audience are smiling. His name is *Karagoz*, or "Black-Eye," and he is a puppet that has been a part of Turkish entertainment since the fourteenth century.

History says that the character of Karagoz first appeared during the fourteenth century. He was rude, illiterate, and a real troublemaker. His best buddy, Hacivad, was always around to get him into trouble. The two of them continue to make up the Turkish entertainment of shadow puppet theater.

A stage is set and then a muslin curtain is hung in front. An oil lamp is placed behind the stage. When the puppets come out, their shadows show up against the curtain sharp and clear. The puppeteer is called a *karagozcu*, and he works all of the puppets alone. His assistant hands him the puppets, while the *yardak* sings the songs that are part of the story and the *dairezen* plays the tambourine. Each play is in four parts, and they always include a fight.

The puppets are made out of camel or water-buffalo hides that are cut and painted. Each one is about 10 to 12 inches (25 to 30 cm) tall. Each story features Karagoz and Hacivad, but other characters are frequently involved also.

Today, these shadow puppet plays are performed primarily for children. Even though other forms of entertainment have come along for kids, these plays are still popular. A school in Bursa continues to teach the art to future puppeteers.

Life in a Turkish Family

Many customs within a Turk's social relationships may seem old-fashioned to people of Western cultures. For instance, when a baby is born in Turkey, it is typical for the mother and child to remain in the home for forty days, so the baby is not exposed to evil spirits. Visitors come by with gifts, but the child stays inside the house. Male children continue to be valued over female children, but this is slowly starting to change.

The tradition of parents selecting a husband or wife for their children is still practiced in parts of Turkey. It is more common in small towns and villages than in large, more modern cities. Many young adults choose their own spouses, but the families must still get together so that the boy's family can formally request permission to ask for the girl's hand in marriage from her parents.

Turkish boys

The roles of women have been changing in Turkey as they are given more rights and educational opportunities. Before Atatürk, most women had few to no civil rights. They weren't

Thinking Ahead

Mothers in Turkey begin gathering and making items for their daughter's wedding trousseau from birth. These napkins, linens, towels, underwear, and more are stored for her future marriage until the girl reaches the age of seventeen.

Fathers, on the other hand, prepare for their son's future weddings by putting away money for a marriage party. They also use the money to help pay for the furniture that the newly wed couple will need. A Turkish marriage is truly a family affair, including everyone.

allowed to vote, and it was very difficult for a woman to get a divorce. All this has changed, yet despite the progress, Turks still carry a strong concept of *hanum hanimcik kadin*, the "womanly woman," and *erkek adam*, the "manly man." The woman is expected to be shy and quiet and to realize that her place is in the home. Even if she holds a job outside the home, the home should remain her first priority. The man is supposed to be brave, loud, emotionless, and fearless.

While Westerners might see telling a woman her place is in the home as oppressive or unfair, for many less-educated Turkish women, this tradition offers power and control. The household is entirely theirs, and they neither expect nor want any help from their spouse. If a man's home is his castle, in Turkey, a woman's home is her entire kingdom to rule.

A Turkish home

Children are very much seen and heard in Turkey. Many schools work on a shift system, so children are often out and about at all times of the day. Turkey has a high birthrate, with seven to ten children to a family common in the less-developed rural areas. Families in the cities have fewer children. Children from wealthier families are often pampered and waited on, but poor children are more apt to fill up their nonschool hours with jobs like polishing shoes, washing car windows, carrying groceries, and selling newspapers. Children live at home with their parents until marriage.

It is not unusual to see children out and about during the day.

The elderly are well taken care of by their families.

When Turkish people grow older, instead of going into an assisted-living area or a nursing home as they do in some cultures, most go to live with their children. They help with household chores if they can, or they may take over a great deal of the child care.

When the elderly pass away, their death is announced in the newspaper. If the person was well known and well liked, these announcements may fill up one or more pages of the local papers. Funerals are generally held in mosques. The *imam*, an Islamic holy person, reads an excerpt from the Qur'an. A dinner is held afterward for the imam, relatives, neighbors, and friends.

Daily Life
in Turkey

1914

1914

D AILY LIFE IN TURKEY HAS CHANGED QUITE A BIT SINCE 1923, when it began to move toward a less religiously based and more modern model. This change has affected everything, from what people wear to where they live.

Opposite: **Daily life in Turkey can be quite similar to that of other modern countries.**

Home, Sweet Home

The types of homes Turks live in vary with the area of the country in which they live. If they live near the Black Sea, for instance, they usually have thatch-roofed cottages made with timber from the nearby forests. Sometimes these houses are built on stilts in case the sea runs over its boundaries and floods the area. In Thrace and northeastern Anatolia, people tend to live in one-story homes made of concrete blocks, while southern and western Anatolia residents have homes made of stone. Central Anatolia, on the other hand, features flat-roofed houses made of sun-dried brick. The wealthy often have concrete-block homes or apartments in suburban areas, and people from the middle class live in apartments, too.

This Turkish home has piles of hay on top.

Housing Problems

When the migration from Turkish villages to big cities continued to climb, it was impossible to avoid a shortage of housing. People kept coming, and there simply were not enough places for them to live. A solution was found by creating squatter settlements outside the cities. The quickly built shacks became shantytowns, or *gecekondu* ("built in the night"), as the Turks call them. Some sources report that today, half of the big cities' residents live in these shacks. For people living in the shantytowns, life is difficult.

Prior to the 1920s, the Kurds, a strong minority within Turkey, lived primarily in tribal groups in rather isolated communities. However, when Atatürk came into power, he wanted the government to force the Kurds to abandon their beliefs in simple living and growing only what they needed to eat. Needless to say, this caused tension within the Kurdish community. The Kurds did not want to be assimilated, or merged with the dominant group. They revolted several times during the 1920s and 1930s, and a number of them gave their lives in the struggle. Today, they still live in Turkey and neighboring countries. Most of them live near one another to maintain traditions.

Time to Eat

Anyone who lives in or visits Turkey had better like lamb, rice, and tea, because these are the basic ingredients of the Turks' daily diet. When people think of Turkish food, they often think of shish kabob, most commonly consisting of chunks of lamb with tomatoes, onions, and peppers grilled on a skewer. While this is a typical dish, daily meals will more likely center on cracked-wheat bread, yogurt, and eggplant.

This street vendor offers berry juice on a hot day.

Some other popular dishes include *pide*, which is like a flat-bread pizza with vegetables, ground lamb, sausage, cheese, or eggs on top; *dolma*, vegetables stuffed with rice, meat, or a mixture of both; and *pilaf*, a combination of rice, almonds, meat, raisins, cheese, and black olives. Dessert might be rice pudding; *borek*, a flaky pastry stuffed with meat and/or cheese; or *baklava*, another type of pastry made with layers of thin dough, honey, and chopped nuts. Drinks vary from coffee and tea to fruit juices to *raki*, a very strong liquor made from grapes. Special treats include *kabak tatlisi*, or very sweet pumpkin pudding with walnuts, or *lokma*, balls of dough deep-fried in sugar syrup.

Other types of foods can be bought on the streets of Turkey. Fresh almonds are sold on carts that can be moved from one corner to another. In the winter, roasted chestnuts can also be purchased. Different sandwich fillings are wrapped in a wheat pancake, and a snack called *simit*, which is sesame-covered bread rings, is popular. Some of the more exotic offerings include grilled sheep's intestines served sandwich-style, and a drink made out of pickle juice.

Sesame rings are a favorite snack.

With all the water surrounding their land, Turks do enjoy eating seafood, including octopus salad, fried mussels, and fried squid. They also place quite an emphasis on fruits and vegetables. They sometimes buy these in great quantities when they are fresh so that they can be dried and preserved for the long winter months ahead. Vegetables are pickled, while jams are made from rose petals, figs, and morello cherries.

Good Table Manners

Table manners in Turkey are different than those in the United States. Before people begin to eat, the host will say *"Afiyet olsun,"* which means "May it be healthy." Wine is often present at the table, and the host always takes the first sip. The host says *"Serefinize,"* meaning "To your good honor," and the guests reply *"Elinize saglik,"* meaning "Health to your hands." It is their way of thanking their host for the food.

When company comes over for dinner, the host does not sit down with the guests. Instead, he or she remains standing to serve them from each dish. When a second helping is offered, the guest is supposed to say no at first, and then give in. Reaching across the table is very acceptable.

Meals are usually served with the small dishes first; followed by a main dish of meat, salad, and a starch; then a second main course of cold cooked vegetables. Turks tend to have a sweet tooth and are known for their desserts. Many meals end with sweets like rice pudding, and then some fresh fruit. When people are finished eating, they place their knives on the right and forks on the left of the plate so that they cross in the middle.

Siskebabi (Turkish Shish Kabob)

1 cup plain yogurt

3 tbs extra-virgin olive oil

3 tbs onion juice (grated from 1 medium-sized onion)

2 lbs boneless lamb cut into cubes

8 10" metal or wooden skewers (pre-soaked in water for 30 minutes)

4 pita breads

Salt and pepper to taste

Method:

Stir together the yogurt, olive oil, and onion juice in a glass or ceramic pan or bowl and season with salt and pepper. Add the lamb cubes, coat with the marinade, and refrigerate, covered, for 4 hours.

Prepare a charcoal fire and let die down a bit or preheat a gas grill for 15 minutes on low. Set the skewers in a skewer holder over the fire and grill until golden brown and succulent, turning often, about 20 minutes. Or, lacking a skewer holder, place them on the grill and grill to perfection. Serve with or on a piece of grilled warm pita bread.

Bread is a staple in a Turk's diet. Some experts estimate that an average Turkish family of four eats three or four loaves of bread every single day!

From Pants to Pantaloons

The casual clothing styles of the West are familiar in the cities of Turkey. Some rural Turks still cling to tradition, with men wearing loose-fitting cloaks and *pantaloons*, or baggy pants. Women's clothing has changed the most as they have gained more rights in their society, but some women still wear scarves on their heads and cover the lower part of their faces in the Islamic tradition of modesty. Mosques require visitors to take off their shoes, and shorts are forbidden inside. Women are expected to cover their heads and shoulders.

School Days

During the Ottoman period, less than 10 percent of the people could read. Now, 85 percent of Turks—the vast majority—are literate by age fifteen. Atatürk strongly believed in the importance of education, and schools were made free.

A Trip to the Grand Bazaar and the Egyptian Spice Market

Turks and foreigners alike appreciate two bazaars located in Istanbul. The *Kapali Carsi*, or Grand Bazaar (above), is more than 500 years old and has more than 4,000 shops, all under one roof. It is the oldest and largest covered marketplace in the world, with twenty-two separate entrances. Walking through it is like walking through a maze. More than 25,000 people work there.

The *Misir Carsi*, or Spice Market (right), on the other hand, is a noisy, crowded place that specializes in selling spices, herbs, fruits, nuts, and candies. Fishers near the waterfront catch fish for customers and cook it right there on charcoal grills. The smell from the cooking and the spices displayed for sale in large burlap bags is amazing.

Daily Life in Turkey **123**

Children study in one of Turkey's public elementary schools.

Children are required by law to start school at age seven and to attend for the next eight years, or until they reach fifteen. After graduation, some students choose to go on to college, while others go to vocational school or into the job world.

As in many other educational systems across the world today, the Turks are working on improvements. They want to make classrooms smaller, and they are beginning to focus their curriculum on computer and foreign-language skills.

Turkish Universities

There are more than fifty public and private universities throughout Turkey. The oldest was founded in 1453. Ankara has four, including Ankara University; Istanbul has nine; Izmir has three; Izmit has two; and the others are scattered across the country. A prestigious university is the American Robert College in Istanbul, which was founded in 1863 by Christopher Robert, a wealthy American industrialist, and Cyrus Hamlin, an American schoolmaster in Babek. Turkey also has a number of foreign high schools in Istanbul and Ankara, including Alman Lisesi-Deutsche Schule and Uskudar American Academy.

Turkish Holidays

New Year's Day	January 1
National Sovereignty and Children's Day	April 23
Youth and Sports Day	May 19
Victory Day	August 30
Republic Day	October 30

A Look at the Media

At last count, there were 635 broadcast stations in Turkey. The programming mainly consists of foreign films, which are dubbed into Turkish, discussion panels, and homemade entertainment shows. There were approximately 21 million televisions in Turkey in 1997.

Private radio stations were not legal until 1994. The Turkish government shut down any that they found, which made the people angry. They began wearing black ribbons on their collars and putting black pieces of material on their cars' antennas in protest. Finally, the government legalized the stations, and by the year 1998, there were more than 90 stations throughout Turkey.

Many magazines and newspapers published in Turkey are quite popular. The biggest-selling newspapers are *Sabah*, *Hurriyet*, *Milliyet*, and *Cumhuriyet*. The conservative newspaper *Turkiye* is quite popular in Turkey, and Ankara has an English-language newspaper called the *Daily News*. *Aktuel* and *Tempo* are the most-read magazines, although businesspeople prefer *Ekonomist* and *Kapital*.

Many people in Turkey cannot afford newspaper and magazine subscriptions. It isn't unusual for children to run alongside a bus or train as it pulls through a station. They aren't begging for money or treats. Instead, they want passengers to throw down the newspapers and magazines they have finished reading so that they can take them home to share with their family.

A sure measure of modernization is a country's high-tech use. As of 2000, there were more than 12 million cell phones

Although still connected to ancient ways, Turkey has welcomed modern amenities.

in use in Turkey. There are more than two dozen Internet providers within Turkey, and more than 2 million Turks use the World Wide Web. These numbers are climbing.

As Turkey moves forward with the rest of the world through the new millennium, its people will continue to benefit from its ancient ruins, its age-old traditions, and the many lessons of its sultans and Atatürk. The people of Turkey will keep blending the old with the new in a way that makes their fascinating country unique.

A Refreshing Tradition

Two thousand years ago, Turkey had more than 100 *hamams*, and today it still has about 100. A hamam is a Turkish bath, and it is a regular part of some Turks' day—and certainly a highlight for visitors.

A Turkish bath is a place to go to get clean, to socialize, and to relax. It is usually made up of three separate rooms, with separate sides for men and women. The first room is called the *camekan*. This is where people come in and change their clothes. The traditional hamam provides a towel, wooden clogs, and a *pestamal*, or sarong. Men wrap these around their waists, and women sometimes wrap them around their upper body. After putting on the pestamal, Turks take showers and then walk through the second room, or *sogukluk*, and into the *hararet*—the hot steam-room.

This is where the most pleasure can be found. Bathers lie face down on their towels on a heated platform and are given a massage. Sometimes they are rubbed down with a camel's hair brush, which is guaranteed to take off at least one layer of dirt—and skin.

Hamams are quite beautiful and commonly feature marble tables, brass fixtures, and awe-inspiring domes. Because the Islamic faith puts such an emphasis on cleanliness, even the poor come to the baths.

Women frequently enjoyed the Turkish baths in the past because they gave them a chance to be in town and to talk with others. Children are usually right alongside their mothers. The hamam is generally the first place a baby is brought after he or she has reached the forty-day mark.

Timeline

Turkish History		World History	
The oldest version of settlements begins in the area known now as Troy.	3000 B.C.		
		2500 B.C.	Egyptians build the Pyramids and the Sphinx in Giza.
Hittites invade Anatolia; this is the first era recorded in written histories.	1500–550 B.C.	563 B.C.	The Buddha is born in India.
Mohammad is born.	570 B.C.		
Cyrus the Great of Persia invades and controls Anatolia for almost 200 years.	546–334 B.C.		
Alexander the great conquers Anatolia.	334–323 B.C.		
The Hagia Sophia is built.	A.D. 325	A.D. 313	The Roman emperor Constantine recognizes Christianity.
Byzantium becomes Constantinople and is made the new capital.	330		
		610	The Prophet Muhammad begins preaching a new religion called Islam.
		1054	The Eastern (Orthodox) and Western (Roman) Churches break apart.
		1066	William the Conqueror defeats the English in the Battle of Hastings.
Byzantium is defeated by the Seljuk Turks at the Battle of Malazgrit. Turkey comes under fifty-seven years of rule by the Crusaders.	1071–1243	1095	Pope Urban II proclaims the First Crusade.
		1215	King John seals the Magna Carta.
The Mongols invade for a brief time.	1243		
The Ottoman Empire officially begins.	1326	1300s	The Renaissance begins in Italy.
		1347	The Black Death sweeps through Europe.
The Ottoman Turks conquer Constantinople; the empire comes into its strongest, most powerful era.	1453	1453	Ottoman Turks capture Constantinople, conquering the Byzantine Empire.
Mimar Koca Sinan is born.	1489		
		1492	Columbus arrives in North America.
		1500s	The Reformation leads to the birth of Protestantism.
		1776	The Declaration of Independence is signed.
		1789	The French Revolution begins.

Turkish History

The Treaty of Adrianpole is signed.	1829
The Ottoman Empire continues to lose territories, including Tunisia, Algeria, and Cyprus.	1830–1881
The first Constitution is adopted.	1876
Turkey enters World War I on the side of the Germans.	1914
Turkey is defeated in World War I and is partly occupied by the Greeks, British, French, and Italians.	1918
The Turkish Grand National Assembly is formed and Kemal is elected president; The Treaty of Sevres is signed.	1920
The Republic of Turkey is made official; Atatürk institutes many changes; the capital is moved to Ankara; The Treaty of Lausanne is signed.	1923
The first Kurdish revolt occurs.	1925
Turkish women are permitted to vote for the first time; Kemal is renamed Atatürk, "Father of the Turks."	1934
The Turkish flag is adopted.	1936
Atatürk dies.	1938
Turkey joins the United Nations and fights on the U.S. side in World War II.	1945
Turkey's first election is held; a transition from single party to multiparty democracy occurs.	1946
Turkey's first free election is held.	1950
Turkey joins NATO.	1952
A second Constitution is established.	1982
Tansu Çiller is elected prime minister.	1993
Ahmet Necdet Sezer is elected president.	2000
An earthquake hits Afyon.	2002

World History

1865	The American Civil War ends.
1914	World War I breaks out.
1917	The Bolshevik Revolution brings communism to Russia.
1929	Worldwide economic depression begins.
1939	World War II begins, following the German invasion of Poland.
1945	World War II ends.
1957	The Vietnam War starts.
1969	Humans land on the moon.
1975	The Vietnam War ends.
1979	Soviet Union invades Afghanistan.
1983	Drought and famine in Africa.
1989	The Berlin Wall is torn down, as communism crumbles in Eastern Europe.
1991	Soviet Union breaks into separate states.
1992	Bill Clinton is elected U.S. president.
2000	George W. Bush is elected U.S. president.

Fast Facts

Official name:	*Turkiye Cumhuriyeti* (Republic of Turkey)
Capital:	Ankara
Official language:	Turkish
Official religion:	None
National anthem:	*Istiklal Marsi* ("The Independence March")

Istanbul

Turkey's flag

Fields and mountains
of Turkey

Government: Republican parliamentary democracy

Chief of state: President

Head of government: Prime minister

Area: 297,614 square miles (770,760 sq km)

Coordinates of geographic center: 39° 00' N, 35° 00' E

Dimensions: 465 miles (748 km) north to south; 1,015 miles (1,633 km) east to west

Bordering countries: Greece, Bulgaria, Georgia, Armenia, Iran, Iraq, Azerbaijan, and Syria

Highest elevation: Mount Ararat, 16,949 feet (5,166 m)

Lowest elevation: Sea level along the Mediterranean Sea

Average temperature: In Ankara, the average temperature in January is 32.5°F (0°C); in July it is 73°F (23°C). Some areas of the country are far colder or hotter.

Average annual rainfall: Around the Black Sea and other coastal areas, rainfall can reach 100 inches (254 cm) a year; the national average is 14.7 inches (37.3 cm).

National population: 67 million

Population of largest cities (1997 est):

Istanbul	9,057,747
Ankara	3,631,612
Izmir	3,066,902
Bursa	1,946,327
Konya	1,943,757
Adana	1,689,155
Antalya	1,477,347

Green Mosque

Currency

Famous landmarks: ▶ *Topkapi Palace, Imperial Treasury, Blue Mosque, Hagia Sophia, Grand Bazaar, and Egyptian Spice Market*, Istanbul

▶ *Museum of Underwater Archaeology*, Bodrum

▶ *Independence War Museum*, Anitkabir, *and Museum of Anatolian Civilization*, Ankara

▶ *Aperlae Island and Kekova Island*, Mediterranean Sea

▶ *Nemrut Mountain and Mount Ararat*, Eastern Turkey

▶ *Green Mosque*, Bursa

▶ *Cappadocia*, Central Anatolia

Industry: Turkey exports and imports goods and products. It trades primarily with Germany, but also with Italy, the United States, Russia, France, and the United Kingdom. Its main imports include chemicals, machinery, petroleum, iron, steel, and motor vehicles, and its main exports are clothing, textiles, cotton, fruits, nuts, wheat, and tobacco. In recent years, the country has spent more on imports (about $56 billion) than it has received from exports (about $27 billion), creating an unfavorable balance of trade. One thing that has helped the economy has been growing tourism within Turkey.

Currency: Turkey's basic unit of currency is the lira. In 2002, 1=U.S.$0.0000007.

Weights and measures: Metric system

Literacy: 85 percent overall

Turkish girls at play

Atatürk (Mustafa Kemal)

Common Turkish words and phrases:

Merhaba.	Hello.
Günaydin.	Good morning.
Iyi geceler.	Good night.
Nasilsiniz?	How are you?
Tesekkurederim.	Thank you.
Allahaismarladik.	Goodbye.
Evet	Yes
Hayir	No
Lütfen	Please
Affedersiniz.	Excuse me.
Turkce bilmiyorum.	I don't speak Turkish.
Anlamiyorum.	I don't understand.
Nerede?	Where is it?
Saatiniz var mi?	What time is it?

Famous Turks:

Atatürk (Mustafa Kemal)   (1881–1938)
Founder of modern Turkey

Aziz Nesin   (1915–1995)
Author

Evliya bin Dervis Mehmet Zilli   (1611–?)
Traveler and writer

Fatih Sultan Mehmet (Mehmet II)   (1432–1481)
Humanist sultan

Mevlana (Celaleddin-i Rumi)   (1204–1273)
Founder of Mevlevi Sufism

Mimar Koca Sinan   (1489–1588)
Ottoman architect

Naim Suleymanoglu   (1967–)
Olympic athlete

Nazim Hikmet   (1902–1963)
Poet

Piri Reis   (1465–1554)
Marine cartographer

Tansu Çiller   (1943–)
First female prime minister

To Find Out More

Fiction

▶ Bagdasarian, Adam. *Forgotten Fire*. United Kingdom: DK Publishing, 2000.

▶ Halvorsen, Lisa. *Letters Home from Turkey*. Woodbridge, Conn.: Blackbirch Marketing, 2000.

▶ Hardy, Tad. *The Mountain That Burns Within*. Colorado Springs, Colo.: Chariot Victor Publishing, 1997.

▶ Thomsen, Paul, and Brian Thompson. *Mystery of the Ark: The Dangerous Journey to Mount Ararat*. Green Forest, Ark.: Master Books, 1997.

▶ Walker, Barbara. *A Treasury of Turkish Folktales for Children*. North Haven, Conn.: Linnet Books, 1998.

▶ Walker, Barbara. *Watermelons, Walnuts, and the Wisdom of Allah and Other Tales of Hoca*. Lubock: Texas Tech University Press, 1991.

Nonfiction

▶ Bator, Robert. *Daily Life in Ancient and Modern Istanbul*. Cities through Time Series. Minneapolis, Minn.: Lerner Publishing, 2000.

▶ Bickman, Connie. *Children of Turkey*. Through the Eyes of Children Series.. Edina, Minn.: Abdo and Daughters Publishing, 1994.

▶ Feinstein, Steve, et al. *Turkey in Pictures*. Minneapolis, Minn.: Lerner Publishing, 1998.

- Kemal, Neriman, et al. *Turkey.* Countries of the World Series. Milwaukee, Wis.: Gareth Stevens Publishing, 2001.

- Lyle, Garry. *Turkey.* Major World Nations Series. Broomall, Pa.: Chelsea House, 1999.

- Sheehan, Sean. *Turkey.* Cultures of the World Series. Tarrytown, N.Y.: Benchmark Books, 1996.

Web Sites

- **Turkey: Crossroads of Civilizations** www.turkey.org *Republic of Turkey's home page. Information about the country, government, economy, culture, travel, and education.*

- **Turkish Daily News** www.turkishdailynews.com *English-language newspaper.*

- **Turkish Odyssey** www.Turkishodyssey.com *Travel and general information.*

Embassy

- **Republic of Turkey Embassy** 2525 Massachusetts Ave., NW Washington, DC, 20008 (202) 612-6700 info@turkey.org

Index

Page numbers in *italics* indicate illustrations.

Meet the Author

TAMRA ORR is a full-time freelance writer and author now living in Portland, Oregon. She spent her first forty years in the Midwest and is now enjoying the beauty of the West Coast. She has written a variety of books for the family, including ones about Korean-American immigration, Native American medicine, and the childhood of Ronald Reagan. In addition to this, she has written a book called A *Parent's Guide to Homeschooling*, writes material for several national educational testing companies, and has had her own column in newspapers and magazines.

Orr graduated from Ball State University in Muncie, Indiana, in 1982 with a bachelor's degree in English and secondary education. She has taught many different classes and workshops, and she also home educates her own four children, ages five to seventeen. "I have the best job in the world," she says. "Between homeschooling and writing, I learn scads of new things every single day."

Writing about Turkey was a wonderful experience for Orr. "I have an all-new respect for the country and the richness of its culture," she says. In the process of writing the book, she tried her hand at making shish kabob and searched the city for some Turkish delight. "Discovering things about other people and how they live," she adds, "gives everyone such an appreciation for what we all have in common and what we can learn from each other." This is her first book for Children's Press.

Photo Credits

Photographs © 2003:

A Perfect Exposure: 41, 96 (Mary Altier), 123 bottom (Randa Bishop), 62 (Sandra Merritt), 92, 105 (Richard T. Nowitz)

AP/Wide World Photos: 102 bottom

Archive Photos/Getty Images/Anatolian/ Reuters: 78, 132 bottom

Art Resource, NY/Erich Lessing: 52

Atlas Geographic/A Perfect Exposure: 10, 20, 23, 33, 35, 36, 40 top, 40 bottom, 43, 44 right, 48, 54, 60, 64, 69, 73, 88, 93 right, 93 left, 99, 104, 107, 111, 113, 121, 132 top

Bridgeman Art Library International Ltd., London/New York/Lauros/Giraudon: 89

Brown Brothers: 56

Buddy Mays/Travel Stock/Donna Carroll: 119

Corbis Images: 98, 108 (AFP), 47 (Archivo Iconografico, S.A.), 49 (Bettmann), 45, 72, 87, 116 (Jonathan Blair), 61 (Jan Butchofsky-Houser), 28 top (Sergei Chirikov/AFP), 2 (Owen Franken), 110 (Chris Hellier), 9 (Dave G. Houser), 14, 24 (Wolfgang Kaehler), 101 (Mike King), 106 (Paul H. Kuiper), 63 left (Reuters NewMedia Inc.), 100 (Jeffrey L. Rottman), 63 right (Tarik Tinazay/AFP), 71, 117 (Nik Wheeler), 18, 34, 127, 131 bottom (Adam Woolfitt)

Corbis Sygma: 70

Dembinsky Photo Assoc.: cover, 6, 30 bottom

Folio, Inc.: 21 (Walter Bibikow), 75 (Jeff Greenberg)

Getty Images/Geoff du Feu: 37

Hulton | Archive/Getty Images: 50, 67, 133 bottom

ImageState: 46 (Roberto Arakaki), 13, 31 (Kadir Kir), 115 (Phyllis Picardi)

MapQuest.com, Inc.: 66 top, 131 top

Mary Evans Picture Library: 57

Peter Arnold Inc.: 83, 130 left (Jeff Greenberg), 26 (Ingeborg Lippmann), 7 bottom, 85 (Robert Mackinlay)

Photo Researchers, NY: 42 (Stephanie Dinkins), 44 left (W. Layer/OKAPIA), 76 (Will & Deni McIntyre)

PhotoEdit: 97, 112 (Jeff Greenberg), 66 bottom (Alan Oddie)

Stock Boston: 90 (Dave Bartruff), 81 (Walter Bibikow), 103 (Michele Burgess), 15 (Rob Crandall), 30 top (Phyllis Picardi)

Stone/Getty Images: 75 (Glen Allison), 7 top, 25 (Thierry Cazabon) 11 (John Lawrence)

The Image Bank/Getty Images/Guido A. Rossi: 123 top

The Image Works: 126 (Arlene Collins), 77 (Rob Crandall), 124 (Margot Granitsas), 8, 120 (Jeff Greenberg), 102 top (Hideo Haga), 68 (Mark Reinstein)

Visuals Unlimited: 79, 80 (Jeff Greenberg), 19 (NASA)

Woodfin Camp & Associates: 114, 133 top (Robert Frerck), 39, 95 (Adam Woolfitt)

Maps by Joe LeMonnier